Unlock your potential today!

COMMUNICATION

The Key to Your **Success**

Master Impactful Communication – Build
Stronger Connections, Overcome Challenges,
and Lead with Confidence

JYOTSNA BIDAVE

ISBN
Paperback 979-8-89610-740-8
Hardcase 979-8-89632-847-6

To my beloved parents...

Whose unwavering love, support, and belief in me have been the foundation of all that I am and will ever be! Aai (Mother), your constant presence by my side and your endless nurturing have shaped my heart; Pappa (Father), your creativity and quiet strength have fuelled my spirit. This book is a tribute to the values you have instilled in me the lessons of love, resilience, and grace.

This book is a humble offering, filled with the love and gratitude I carry for you always!

TABLE OF CONTENT

ACKNOWLEDGMENTS

I express my deepest gratitude to the Universe for blessing me with the ability to create this work. Thanks to all my parents, teachers, and mentors who have contributed in one way or another to making me capable of contributing to this world. A wholehearted thanks to my dearest friends and family members who have been with me on this journey, supporting and encouraging me every step of the way, especially to my husband, Deepak, and my son, Parth, who not only supported but patiently gave me the time and space to complete this book. This work would not have been possible without their presence and support.

My thanks also extend to the books, research articles, blogs, each learning opportunity, and my work experience that helped shape the content of this book. Thank you, Notion Press and the entire team, for your guidance in bringing this book to life. I am deeply thankful for my home support, who seamlessly took on many responsibilities, allowing me to focus on writing, and for all the tools and resources to assist me in bringing my final work to fruition.

Finally, to you dear reader, this book is for you! Thank you for your trust and willingness to explore communication possibilities. May this book become a meaningful part of your journey and inspire growth and transformation in every conversation you have!

PREFACE

I appreciate you picking this book and investing in yourself. Communication is a skill that touches every part of our lives, and by reading these pages, you're taking an essential step toward more profound and meaningful connections.

Throughout this book, you'll notice that I've used second-person narration. This is intentional because I'm directly communicating with you. As you progress through the book, I aim for this to feel like a one-on-one personal dialogue from my heart to yours.

This book is not just about communication; it's about a journey I started in 2007 when I began teaching communication skills. At first, it was simply a subject to teach. However, as I explored further ways to improve my teaching, I realized that communication is an inseparable part of human life. It's often underrated. The more I taught, the more I understood. I delved deeper, experimented more, and grew with each discovery. That journey began years ago and continues today, taking shape in this book's form.

My experiences as a lecturer, trainer, coach, and administrator, along with my various personal and professional roles, have helped me realize the true impact of communication. Over the years, I learned how to communicate effectively and why communication matters in every interaction. What I've gathered through these experiences, I now share with you in this book.

As you read, you'll find this book is more than just ideas; it's an experiential journey. I've poured into these pages what I've learned about communication in every role, from teacher to mentor and even as a lifelong student. Over the years, I've witnessed how clear and purposeful communication can transform relationships and unlock personal potential. I've connected more deeply with each new insight with others and myself. This is my humble attempt to offer you the wisdom I've gained.

Before You Start Reading...

Congratulations! You're embarking on a journey to build a robust foundation for your communication. This book will go beyond explaining communication concepts; it will walk you through practical experiences, emotions, and thoughts related to communication, equipping you with tools you can apply to every area of your life.

Mastering communication is more than a skill you practice here and there. It's a gift and a craft that enriches every relationship you have, including the one with yourself. Communication connects your personal, professional, and even spiritual worlds, helping you live in greater harmony with others and yourself.

There's plenty of material on building success, habits, self, development, positivity, relationships, and spirituality in almost every aspect of life. But knowing something without applying it is ultimately unhelpful. As you move through this book, remember that you're reading to *implement*, practice, and enhance your life experiences. This journey isn't just about reading but putting the ideas into practice. By engaging with each reflection and exercise, you'll see real, lasting change in connecting with others.

I encourage you to engage with the content actively. Keep a pen nearby, take notes, highlight key points, and jot down answers to the questions asked throughout the book. Make this book your own, personal copy filled with your thoughts, observations, and reflections that you can get back to in the future. Let this book be your companion as you improve your communication whether with yourself, your loved ones, or your professional or social life.

I started writing this book after six months of contemplation. I knew it needed to be more than just a collection of ideas. I wanted it to feel like a friend, a guide who listens, understands, and helps you grow. This book is about two things: communication and *you*.

Communication is a profound, though often underrated, part of human life. Language, a gift unique to humans, distinguishes us from all other species. Just think how valuable is this gift of communication? Mastering the art of language to communicate effectively can elevate your life experiences to new heights.

Before we begin, let me tell you that the book is a work in progress. While it's intended to help you deepen your understanding and practice of communication, it may not be 'perfect' in every sense. I welcome your feedback, but I encourage you not to let any imperfections affect your learning process. Embrace the journey and remain open to learning.

The exercises and ideas in this book may sometimes feel overwhelming or even repetitive. That's perfectly okay. You don't need to implement everything at once; start with one practice at a time. Unlike other projects in your life, there are no deadlines here. I took years to learn and adapt to effective communication practices. I intend your journey to be smoother, faster, and more impactful with the support of the experiences I've woven into this book.

This book explores critical concepts around communication that are vital to personal growth. These themes may appear throughout the chapters, sometimes even where the chapter's focus might seem different. These core ideas will resurface as you grow through the material, grounding you and reinforcing the interconnectedness of all aspects of communication.

Whether you're a professional looking to enhance your leadership skills, a parent striving to communicate better with your children, a young adult navigating new relationships, or someone passionate about personal growth, this book is for you. "Communication: The Key to Your Success" is designed to guide you in mastering the art of meaningful dialogue, transforming your inner talk, and building strong, positive connections with those around you. By the end of this journey, you'll understand the profound impact of communication on every aspect of your life and possess the practical tools to transform how you connect with yourself, others, and the world. Whether boosting your professional relationships, deepening your personal bonds, or enhancing your inner clarity, this book will empower you to become a confident communicator and unlock new possibilities in all areas of your life.

Before Moving Ahead...

Take a moment to reflect on the following questions. If it feels helpful, write down your answers:

- What specific communication challenges do you face? Would you like to list them?
- What specific shifts do you hope to experience in your communication as you complete this book?

As you begin, remember that this book is your companion, guiding you through each chapter toward becoming a more effective and authentic communicator. At the end of each part, you'll find situational skill-building exercises designed to deepen your understanding and help you apply the concepts in real-world scenarios.

I want you to approach each chapter with patience and reflection. This book is designed not as a quick read but as a guide for deep and lasting growth. Each chapter builds on essential ideas, with exercises and reflections meant to help you explore these concepts at your own pace. I encourage you to take one chapter at a time, pausing to absorb, reflect, and apply the insights before moving forward. Allow yourself to engage fully with each section, and trust that by embracing this gradual exploration, you'll create a richer, more impactful experience. Remember, growth is a journey; let each chapter be a step toward discovering a more empowered and self, aware version of yourself.

Let's embark on this journey together as you take steps toward becoming the confident, compassionate communicator you aspire to be!

Communication Self-Assessment

As you begin this journey, take a moment to explore your current perspectives and habits around communication. This self-assessment is designed to help you understand your starting point, your strengths, tendencies, and areas where you might grow.

Instructions: Rate yourself from 0 to 5 for each statement, based on how often you demonstrate each behaviour or mindset in your daily life. Be honest with yourself; this isn't about "right" or "wrong" answers but rather a snapshot of where you are right now.

- **0** = Never
- **1** = Rarely
- **2** = Occasionally
- **3** = Sometimes
- **4** = Frequently
- **5** = Always

Let's dive in and understand where you are with your communication today. Enjoy the process!

1. I feel comfortable sharing my thoughts.

       1   **2**   **3**   **4**   **5**

2. I pay attention to my body language and tone.

       1   **2**   **3**   **4**   **5**

3. I try to understand the emotions behind others' words.

       1   **2**   **3**   **4**   **5**

4. I listen without interrupting or planning my response.

       1   **2**   **3**   **4**   **5**

5. I adjust my communication style to fit different people and situations.

       1   **2**   **3**   **4**   **5**

6. I handle difficult conversations calmly.

       1   **2**   **3**   **4**   **5**

7. I am aware of how my inner dialogue affects my communication.

       1   **2**   **3**   **4**   **5**

8. I stay open-minded and try to understand other perspectives.

       1   **2**   **3**   **4**   **5**

9. I make sure my message is clear and understood.

       1   **2**   **3**   **4**   **5**

10. I seek feedback on my communication and try to improve.

        1   **2**   **3**   **4**   **5**

11. I see communication as a skill I can always improve.

        1   **2**   **3**   **4**   **5**

12. I manage my emotions well during conversations.

        1   **2**   **3**   **4**   **5**

13. I consider the impact of my words before speaking.

    1   2   3   4   5

14. I listen with curiosity, not judgment.

    1   2   3   4   5

15. I use words and Non-verbal cues to communicate my message.

    1   2   3   4   5

INTRODUCTION: UNLOCKING THE POWER OF COMMUNICATION

"The single biggest problem in communication is the illusion that it has taken place."

— George Bernard Shaw

Have you ever been in a conversation where the other person wasn't listening? Or maybe you found yourself explaining something repeatedly, yet your message didn't seem to land? Despite its central role, we often take communication for granted. We speak daily, whether in casual chats, work meetings, or meaningful conversations, but how frequently do we pause to consider whether we communicate effectively?

In today's fast, paced world, where digital communication dominates, connecting genuinely through conversation can feel more challenging than ever. Social media, emails, and texts make it easier to communicate quickly but often create barriers to proper understanding. This book is an invitation to help you close that gap. *Communication: The Key to Your Success* explores the deeper layers of communication beyond just speaking and listening. Whether you're a leader hoping to inspire your team, a parent looking to connect with your children, or someone seeking to improve relationships, this book will guide you in refining your most potent tool: communication.

The Internal Dialogue: Where Communication Begins

Our conversations with ourselves and our inner dialogue often go unnoticed in communication. Yet, this internal dialogue shapes every interaction we have with others. If self-talk is filled with doubt or negativity, it impacts our external communication. We may second-guess our words, hesitate, or avoid difficult conversations altogether.

In contrast, an empowering and constructive inner dialogue brings confidence and clarity to our interactions. Throughout this book, you'll find exercises to help you reflect on your internal dialogue, identify any patterns holding you back, and cultivate more positive self-talk. Developing a healthy relationship with yourself will unlock the key to becoming a confident and effective communicator.

Let me share my experience of embracing communication in my life. Trust me, I was no different from many of you. I was incredibly shy and often held back my expressions, finding it difficult to voice my viewpoints, even when I knew I was right. This lack of confidence created numerous challenges in my personal and professional life.

However, as I grew in my understanding of communication and developed greater self-awareness, I started taking slow, steady, and conscious steps toward change. Through practice and reflection, I gradually transformed my ability to communicate effectively. Today, I stand here, empowered and confident, and I am excited to share the insights I've gained along this journey with you.

Why Communication Matters

At its heart, communication is about connection. It's the bridge linking people, ideas, and actions. It's how we express who we are, what we think, and how we feel. Yet, as Shaw insightfully pointed out, communication is often an illusion. We assume that because we're speaking, we're being understood. But effective communication goes beyond words; it's about intent, clarity, and empathy. It's about ensuring that you are heard and hear others. It's the ability to bridge the gap between different perspectives and find common ground.

Here's the secret: communication isn't just what you say; it's how you say it; your tone of voice, body language, and framing of the message all play interconnected roles. By focusing on these elements, you'll convey your thoughts effectively and build trust, resolve conflicts, and foster mutual understanding.

The Foundation of Effective Communication: Understanding What, How, and Why

At the heart of powerful communication lies a simple yet transformative framework: understanding the *what, how,* and *why* of every message you convey. Before diving into the specifics of communication skills, we must ground ourselves in these three questions, which will serve as the foundation for clarity, purpose, and connection throughout this book.

- **What**: Identifying the core message and what you need to say ensures that your communication is focused and impactful.

- **How**: Choosing how to deliver the message, including tone, body language, and words, allows you to communicate clearly and appropriately for your audience.

- **Why**: Knowing the purpose behind your message gives it meaning and relevance, guiding your approach and helping you connect more deeply.

The 'What' of Communication

What is in communication is about content determining precisely what information you need to convey to ensure understanding.

It's important to distil your message into core points, making it concise and relevant.

- **Key Messages**: Start by identifying the central message or the most critical information. By pinpointing these, you avoid information overload and can keep the conversation focused.

- **Avoiding Overload**: In effective communication, less is often more. Avoid overwhelming your audience with details that aren't essential to the core message.

If you're presenting an update on a project, focus on critical milestones, current status, and any challenges that need attention. Less essential details, like minor adjustments or smaller team updates, can be saved for a written follow-up. This keeps your audience engaged and avoids unnecessary complexity.

The 'How' of Communication

The *how* refers to the method and style of delivery of how you choose to express your message. It encompasses tone, body language, and word choice, which ensure the message lands effectively.

- **Tone and Approach**: Adjusting your tone based on who you're speaking to can make all the difference. Formality, empathy, and enthusiasm should be calibrated to suit the audience and context.

- **Non-verbal Communication**: Your body language, eye contact, and gestures communicate as much as your words. Ensuring these Non-verbal cues align with your message strengthens credibility and connection.

- **Language Choice**: Choosing words your audience will understand and relate to is essential for clarity.

- **Choosing the Right Medium/Channel**: The same message can be conveyed through different channels like a speech, a presentation, a meeting, a phone call, a text message or an email. Selecting the right medium or channel determines how effectively the message has been conveyed.

Let's say you're explaining a technical concept to someone new to the topic. Instead of using jargon or complex terms, simplify the language to make it approachable. Here, you would be mindful of your channels. You could use audio and visuals to make the concepts easy to understand. Contrast this with explaining the same idea to an industry expert, where technical vocabulary might be expected and appreciated. Here. You might want to make it more significant to them by giving relatable examples or case studies.

The 'Why' of Communication

The *why* is the purpose behind your message. Knowing why you're communicating clarifies your intent, aligns the conversation, and makes the message more meaningful for you and your audience.

- **Guiding Questions**:
  - Why does this message matter?
  - Why are you sharing this message?
  - Why are you choosing the form and channel for the message with the particular audience?
  - What impact or change do you hope to achieve by sharing this information?

Imagine motivating your team for an important project. Emphasising the *why* and how the project aligns with the organisation's goals and benefits, each team member can increase buy-in and inspire commitment. When people understand the significance, they are more likely to engage fully and positively.

Integrating What, How, and Why for Impactful Communication

Combining what, how, and why creates a holistic approach that drives clarity and connection. This framework ensures that every part of your message supports a cohesive, practical outcome.

- **Steps to Combine**:
    - **Define your message (What)**: Write down the core points you must convey.
    - **Decide on delivery (How)**: Plan how you'll say it, considering tone, Non-verbal cues, and clarity of language.
    - **Identify purpose (Why)**: Remind yourself of the reason for the conversation to align your approach with this intention.

Think of a personal or professional message you need to deliver soon. Ask yourself:

1. What is the core message I want to communicate?
2. How can I best convey it for clarity and engagement?
3. Why is it important to communicate this message now, and what change do I hope to see?

Jot down your answers and reflect on how this approach shapes your message. Practicing this framework will make it easier to apply naturally in future conversations.

What you'll Gain from This Book

By the end of this journey, you'll have a deeper, more nuanced understanding of communication that goes far beyond merely speaking or listening. You'll gain tools to:

- *Communicate with Confidence*: Whether you're presenting, leading, or having meaningful conversations, you'll develop the skills to express yourself clearly and assertively.

- *Master the Art of Listening and Empathy*: Become an active listener, giving others your full attention and gaining a deeper understanding of their perspectives.

- *Handle Difficult Conversations with Grace*: Approach conflicts with empathy, turning challenges into opportunities for growth and connection.

- *Build Stronger Relationships*: Effective communication fosters trust and connection, enhancing personal and professional relationships.

- *Refine Non-verbal Skills*: Discover how body language, tone, and facial expressions can complement your message and strengthen understanding.

- *Communicate with Compassion and Assertion*: Learn to blend compassion with confidence, creating more meaningful, impactful interactions.

- *Develop Authentic, Integrity, and Driven Communication*: Engage in conversations that reflect your true self, aligning your words and actions with your values.

You will learn effective communication in the modern world with Humour, Storytelling, Clarity and Intention. Negotiations will better your personal and professional lives. More importantly, you will watch yourself leading through this journey step by step reaching to the pinnacle!

The Path to Mastery

Communication is not something that can be mastered overnight. It takes practice, patience, and a commitment to growth. The tools and strategies in this book are designed to be practical and actionable so that you can apply them in your daily life. Communication is a journey, not a destination.

Stay open and reflective. Note your strengths and areas for growth. Each interaction is an opportunity to learn and improve. Use these insights to build stronger, more meaningful connections with those around you.

Are you ready to unlock the true power of communication?

PART 1

**FOUNDATIONS OF
EFFECTIVE COMMUNICATION**

"The beginning of wisdom is the definition of terms."

— Socrates.

Welcome to the first step of our journey; a deep exploration of the essential building blocks of communication. In this part, we'll uncover the core elements that shape every interaction, from the subtle nuances of unspoken cues to the transformative power of active listening. Consider this section your guide to understanding what makes communication effective and impactful.

Have you ever wondered why some conversations flow effortlessly while others feel strained? Or why certain words and gestures can strengthen bonds while others create distance? This section invites you to reflect inward and explore how your perceptions, habits, and intentions influence your interactions. Developing this awareness will lay the groundwork for more authentic, transparent, and meaningful connections.

Through these chapters, you'll delve into practical insights and tools that help you rediscover the basics of communication, which often goes unnoticed but is profoundly influential. Each chapter equips you with actionable steps to enhance your communication skills, from interpreting body language to mastering the often-forgotten art of listening.

Effective communication starts with clarity within yourself and with others. Understanding your unique communication style and learning to recognize subtle cues in interactions will build a strong foundation for meaningful relationships in every aspect of your life. This is where your journey begins, unlocking the potential for deeper connections and authentic expression.

Chapter 1

WHAT DOES COMMUNICATION MEAN TO YOU?

"You cannot not communicate."

— Paul Watzlawick

Communication is not optional; it's a constant, intrinsic part of being human. Every word, action, and even inaction conveys a message from the moment we wake to the time we sleep. Have you ever thought about how even silence speaks? Whether you choose to engage or withdraw, your behaviour communicates volumes.

If you decide not to respond to someone, your silence alone delivers a message. Whether intentional or not, you're always communicating. The interplay of words and gestures shapes our connections, emotions, and relationships. The concept of *Garbh Sanskar* in Indian culture beautifully illustrates this. Even a baby in the womb absorbs the vibrations of its surroundings, showcasing that communication begins long before birth and continues until our final breath.

This lifelong process is why communication deserves our conscious attention. Everything around us speaks to us if we pause to notice. The unwatered plants on a balcony signal neglect, while a messy kitchen after work silently narrates an incomplete day. These moments emphasize that communication is not just spoken words but a way of perceiving and interacting with the world around us.

Communication as an Inseparable Part of Human Life

Communication manifests in countless ways, often without us realizing it. Every glance, gesture, or decision not to engage carries meaning. Consider these examples:

1. **Avoiding Eye Contact:** Imagine someone avoiding your gaze during a conversation. It might suggest discomfort or disinterest, even if unintentional.

2. **Body Language:** A defensive stance, such as crossed arms, can signal unwillingness to engage, even when words say otherwise.

3. **Silence:** Silence is a potent communicator. Whether used intentionally or unintentionally, it can convey disappointment, anger, or exhaustion.

4. **Non-Responsiveness:** Ignoring messages or calls doesn't just signal busyness, it communicates priorities or emotions about the sender.

5. **Facial Expressions:** A smile in passing conveys warmth and friendliness, while a frown might suggest dissatisfaction or frustration.

Every action or inaction is a form of expression, shaping how others perceive and respond to us. Communication is as natural as breathing, yet we often overlook its significance.

An Unexpected Lesson in Silence

During one of my law classes, I learned a profound lesson about silence. Faced with a noisy classroom, I could have raised my voice to demand quiet, but instead, I chose stillness. I stood at the centre of the room, silent and steady. Slowly, students began nudging each other to focus.

Within moments, the room fell silent, not from commands but from the sheer power of my non-verbal cues. This approach taught me that communication doesn't always require words. Sometimes, the absence of speech can create a substantial impact.

At Its Core

At its essence, communication goes beyond words. It encompasses tone, body language, and listening, all of which contribute to building genuine understanding. Imagine how your tone changes when speaking with a friend versus addressing a professional audience. Each interaction reflects who you are and creates connections that form the foundation of your relationships.

Miscommunication in the Workplace

Miscommunication often stems from unspoken assumptions or unclear expectations. Consider John, a software developer, who responded to a supervisor's email requesting a "quick update" with a brief summary. The supervisor, expecting a detailed report, felt frustrated.

What went wrong? The lack of clarity. After the incident, John began asking clarifying questions, significantly improving workplace interactions. This small shift demonstrates the importance of clear and intentional communication.

Reflecting on my first job, I learned this lesson the hard way. As a shy lecturer intimidated by senior faculty, I hesitated to ask essential questions. By the end of the semester, I realized how crucial it was to overcome my fears and seek clarity. I've learned that communication isn't just about speaking but also knowing when to ask and listen.

Two Different Approaches to Communication

Let's consider two contrasting communication styles:

1. **Sarah:** Direct and task-oriented, Sarah values efficiency. While this approach works in fast-paced environments, it often leaves people feeling dismissed or unimportant.

2. **John:** Empathetic and attentive; John listens carefully and asks meaningful questions, building trust and strong relationships.

Neither approach is inherently wrong, but your communication style shapes how others perceive and respond to you. Recognizing this can help you adjust your style to suit different situations and goals.

Summary

This chapter established communication as an inherent and dynamic aspect of human life. It illustrated how communication extends beyond words, including silence, body language, and inaction. With examples and insights, readers were encouraged to recognize communication's omnipresence and role in building connections, fostering understanding, and navigating challenges.

Key Takeaways

- Communication is an unavoidable part of life, encompassing words, actions, and even silence.

- Understanding your communication habits helps you grow and connect more effectively.

- Intentional and clear communication prevents misunderstandings and fosters stronger relationships.

Reflection Activity

- Think of a recent interaction. Was your communication clear and effective? What might you have done differently?

- Reflect on your communication style. Are you more like Sarah or John? How can you balance directness with empathy?

Self-Assessment Checklist

Rate yourself from 0 (Rarely) to 5 (All the time):

1. I recognize the importance of communication in daily interactions. ___ / 5

2. I actively listen without planning my response while the other person is speaking. ___ / 5

3. I express my thoughts and feelings assertively, communicating my needs effectively. ___ / 5

4. I empathize with and seek to understand the other person's perspective. ___ / 5

5. I am mindful of the intent behind my communication and ensure my tone and body language match my message. ___ / 5

Chapter 2

AUDIENCE AND FEEDBACK: ESSENTIAL ELEMENTS FOR EFFECTIVE INTERACTION

"We all need people who will give us feedback. That's how we improve."

—Bill Gates.

Knowing your audience is a core part of effective communication. Truly connecting with others goes beyond just expressing yourself; it involves understanding who you're speaking to and actively seeking feedback to create a meaningful interaction. Have you ever thought carefully about your audience before communicating? Consider this scenario: imagine you missed an important lecture. How would you explain it to different people? You might tell a friend, "I skipped it today; it was a bit dull, and I needed a break." But to your mother, you'd say, "I felt overwhelmed and needed some time off." And to your professor, you'd explain, "I'm sorry I missed the lecture, but I'll catch up." The story remains the same, yet your approach shifts depending on who you're speaking to.

Same is the case of feedback. Any successful person or organisation has grown because they have constantly sought feedback and improved themselves. This chapter delves into why understanding your audience and embracing feedback are vital for effective communication, helping you approach every interaction with intention and awareness.

Audience-Centric Communication

Audience-centric communication means focusing on what the audience needs to hear, how they need to listen, and what they will find most valuable. Studies in communication psychology emphasize that people are more receptive when the message aligns with their expectations, needs, and values. As renowned communication expert Dale Carnegie once said, "Talk to someone about themselves, and they'll listen for hours." This quote highlights that effective communication isn't about the speaker but the audience and their priorities. When you make the audience feel seen and valued, you build trust and receptivity.

Imagine preparing a project proposal for a client. When you understand the client's priorities, you can shape your message to highlight aspects they care about, such as the timeline, budget, or project impact. Instead of delving into technical details, focusing on what matters most to them increases the likelihood of a positive response and builds a strong foundation for collaboration. For example, if the client prioritizes cost efficiency, you could emphasize budget strategies rather than technical specifications, making them feel you genuinely understand their needs.

Adapting Communication goes beyond merely choosing different words; it's about creating a connection that meets the unique preferences of each audience. Picture Alex, a marketing manager, presenting a product launch strategy to two distinct groups: executives and the marketing team. He uses a formal tone for the executives, emphasizing data, market trends, and high-level strategy. He adopts a collaborative tone for the marketing team, inviting questions, using informal language, and focusing on creativity. This personalized approach ensures that his message resonates with both audiences, reinforcing the importance of a tailored approach to communication.

Research from Stanford University shows that people remember messages better when they're tailored to their specific interests or concerns. This "audience-centered" model of communication can increase engagement and message retention by up to 60%. Alex's tailored approach demonstrates this in practice, ensuring both teams walk away with a clear understanding of the product launch, feeling both informed and involved.

By aligning communication to the audience's unique needs, we create connections, foster understanding, and improve the likelihood of achieving positive outcomes. Audience-centric communication is not only an art but a science grounded in the psychology of effective interpersonal connection.

Feedback as the Communication Loop

Feedback is essential for effective communication because it completes the communication loop, confirming whether your message has been received as intended. It offers an opportunity to adjust and improve clarity. Without feedback, communication risks becoming a one-sided process prone to misunderstandings.

Feedback can be verbal or non-verbal, direct or indirect. Imagine giving a presentation and noticing that your audience appears confused. This Non-verbal feedback is a cue to clarify your points or provide more context. Feedback can be as subtle as body language, facial expressions, or the general energy in the room. Observing these cues allows you to adapt your communication in real-time.

Constructive Feedback

Constructive feedback is vital for growth, both personally and professionally. Actively seeking feedback, asking questions like,

"Did this make sense?" or "What could I have explained better?" shows a willingness to learn and improve. Constructive feedback helps refine your approach, keeping your communication effective and impactful.

Consider a classroom where a teacher asks students, "Which parts of today's lesson were challenging?" By seeking feedback, the teacher gains insight into which sections may need more focus, ensuring everyone understands clearly. Even in personal interactions, constructive feedback can clarify misunderstandings, build stronger relationships, and maintain a positive environment.

Remember when you have received feedback, perhaps after a course or customer service interaction. Thoughtfully crafted feedback requests make us feel valued, as they express a genuine interest in improvement. The same principle applies to workplace and personal relationships. Receiving feedback may sometimes feel daunting, but it's an essential step toward growth.

For example, when I moved to Mumbai from a small town, I realized my colleagues spoke more fluent English. Rather than shying away, I asked for feedback and learned from them. Within months, I was speaking better without feeling different from my colleagues. Feedback created that transformation.

In another scenario, a project manager, Lina, noticed her team members were hesitant to share ideas. After gathering feedback, she learned they felt undervalued. Lina then prioritized inviting input explicitly and acknowledging everyone's contributions, creating a more engaged and collaborative team environment. This example highlights how feedback can remove obstacles and foster productivity.

Feedback is equally important in personal relations. If you think someone in your family or friends is not being usual, seek feedback and see how it transforms your relationship with them.

During their recent conversations, Meera had noticed that her usually cheerful friend, Kavya, seemed distant and quieter than usual. Instead of assuming Kavya was busy or uninterested, Meera gently sought feedback. One evening, over coffee, Meera shared her feelings, saying, "I've noticed you seem a bit quieter than usual lately. Is everything alright?"

To Meera's surprise, Kavya opened up, sharing that she felt overwhelmed with work and personal commitments. She admitted she hadn't reached out because she didn't want to burden anyone. Meera listened attentively, offering support and reassurance, letting Kavya know that her presence and friendship mattered deeply.

This simple moment of seeking feedback transformed their relationship. Kavya felt understood and valued, and Meera gained a deeper insight into her friend's life. What could have led to a widening gap in their friendship became an opportunity to reconnect and strengthen their bond. Through that one act of seeking feedback, Meera showed Kavya that she was willing to listen and offer support, a gesture that communicated care far beyond words.

If Meera had not addressed the change she sensed in Kavya, their friendship would likely have grown more distant over time. Misunderstandings or feelings of neglect could have set in, causing each of them to drift apart. By taking the initiative to seek feedback, Meera reinforced their connection and created a space for open, honest communication that strengthened their bond for the future.

Practical Steps for Effective Audience and Feedback, Centric Communication

- *Know Your Audience*: Understand who you speak to before initiating a conversation or presentation. Consider what they value and their knowledge level of the topic.

- *Adapt Your Message*: Adjust tone, language, and depth to match the audience, enhancing the relevance and resonance of your message.

- *Encourage Feedback*: Invite feedback through questions, observing body language, and openness to responses.

- *Act on Feedback*: Use received feedback to refine your approach, enhancing clarity and alignment with your audience's needs.

- *Practise Empathy*: Step into your audience's perspective to ensure your message is accessible and relevant to them.

The Power of Audience and Feedback

Effective communication is more than expressing your thoughts; it's about connecting with your audience and confirming that your message has been understood. Understanding your audience and actively seeking feedback is essential for successful interactions. Adapting communication to audience needs and integrating feedback creates a continuous improvement cycle, enhancing clarity and engagement.

I cannot envision growth in life without embracing feedback and understanding my audience. Over the years, I've discovered how transformative this can be, not just in teaching, where I've adapted the same syllabus in entirely different ways to suit the unique dynamics of various classes but in every role I play. Whether as a mother, wife, daughter, friend, teacher, coach, meditator, or writer, I tailor my communication and actions based on who I'm engaging with. I consciously choose my words carefully, always seeking feedback with a growth mindset. This isn't limited to others; through self-observation, I consistently give feedback to myself. In doing so, I evolve continuously in both small, everyday moments and larger life decisions, ensuring I grow personally, professionally, socially, and spiritually.

Summary

This chapter explores the importance of understanding your audience and incorporating feedback to enhance communication. Effective communication is dynamic and adapts to the audience's needs, tone, and context to ensure the message resonates. Whether verbal or non-verbal, feedback completes the communication loop, confirming that the message is clear and understood. Audience, centered communication and constructive feedback are powerful tools for improving clarity, connection, and engagement.

Key Takeaways

- **Understand Your Audience**: Effective communication requires a keen understanding of the audience's needs, expectations, and preferences.

- **Adapt Communication**: Tailor tone, language, and content to suit your audience.

- **Feedback Completes Communication**: Feedback is essential for ensuring the clarity and effectiveness of your message.

- **Constructive Feedback is Key**: Seeking and offering constructive feedback fosters continuous improvement and understanding.

- **Empathy Matters**: Considering your audience's perspective enhances message accessibility and relevance.

Reflection Activity

Take a moment to think about your recent interactions:

- Did you adapt your communication based on your audience's needs and expectations?

- How did the audience respond, and what type of feedback (verbal or non-verbal) did you receive?

- Before your next significant conversation, consider what adjustments might improve your connection with the audience.

- Think of a time when you received feedback that helped improve your communication. What was the feedback, and how did you incorporate it into your future interactions?

Self-Assessment Checklist

Evaluate your current communication habits on a scale from 0 (Not at all) to 5 (All the time):

1. I adapt my message based on who I am communicating with. ___ / 5

2. I actively seek feedback after important conversations or presentations. ___ / 5

3. I observe my audience's Non-verbal cues and adjust accordingly. ___ / 5

4. I provide constructive feedback to others in a respectful way. ___ / 5

5. I think about my audience's needs before starting a conversation. ___ / 5

Chapter 3

LISTENING: THE FORGOTTEN ART

*"Most people do not listen with the intent to understand;
they listen with the intent to reply."*

—Stephen R. Covey

Listening is one of the most crucial yet often neglected aspects of communication. It goes beyond just hearing words; it's about genuinely connecting, understanding, and engaging with others. Stephen R. Covey's quote reminds us that we often focus on what we want to say rather than truly understanding the other person.

Research from Harvard University's Social Psychology department supports this, showing that active listening, which involves entirely focusing, understanding, and responding thoughtfully, strengthens trust and rapport in relationships. In his book *The Lost Art of Listening*, Dr. Michael P. Nichols explains that when people feel genuinely heard, it can dissolve tensions and create a foundation of respect and empathy. I have many people who love me dearly, yet I sometimes think they don't listen. Sometimes, it feels like they're just waiting for their turn to respond or give advice rather than taking in what I'm trying to share. It leaves me feeling unheard and sometimes even misunderstood. How many times have you felt this way? Now, take a moment to think about who you prefer sharing your thoughts with. Chances are, it's someone who has the patience and presence to listen to you without interruption.

In this chapter, we'll explore why listening is a forgotten art, the critical differences between hearing and truly listening, and how mastering the skill of listening can transform our relationships and interactions. By the end, you'll understand how this essential skill can create deeper connections and more meaningful conversations.

Is Listening a Skill?

Listening might seem like something that comes naturally, and because of this, we often overlook it as a skill that needs to be learned and practised. Unlike speaking or writing, which are refined through education, listening is assumed to happen automatically. However, genuinely effective listening requires conscious effort and continuous improvement.

Listening is essential for personal and professional growth. In our personal lives, good listening builds trust, deepens relationships, and prevents misunderstandings. Professionally, listening is a critical part of leadership, teamwork, and client relationships. Whether you're leading a team, negotiating a deal, or comforting a friend, developing your listening skills can make all the difference in how successful and meaningful those interactions are.

Imagine you're telling a friend about a stressful day, but halfway through, they interrupt with their own story, barely acknowledging yours. How does that feel? Most of us have been on both sides of this interaction: talking but not feeling heard and listening but not fully present. Stephen R. Covey's quote perfectly captures this common struggle. Instead of genuinely listening to understand, we often listen just to respond.

Listening has become a forgotten art in today's fast-paced, distracted, filled world. With constant notifications, social media, and the pressure to multitask, genuine listening, which builds understanding and connection, has become rare. Listening is more than waiting for your turn to talk; it's an active, empathetic process that requires presence, attentiveness, and openness to the speaker's perspective. In this chapter, we'll explore why listening is so vital, the key differences between hearing and listening, and how cultivating the art of listening can transform your relationships and overall communication.

The Difference between Hearing and Listening

At first glance, hearing and listening may seem like the same thing. Both involve perceiving sound. However, the difference between the two is critical: *hearing* is passive, while *listening* is active. Hearing happens automatically. It's an involuntary function; you always hear sounds, from honking cars to background chatter. But listening requires intentionality. It's about focusing your attention, absorbing the message, and being fully present in the conversation. Simply put, hearing is the reception of sound, while listening is the understanding of meaning.

Before discussing listening skills in my lectures, I would show students an engaging and informative video. They enjoyed it, but when I asked factual questions afterward, only a small percentage could answer. Then, after explaining the importance of listening, I would show another video, this time instructing them to pay close attention as I asked questions based on it. Almost all students answered correctly. This simple exercise illustrated the difference between passive and active listening.

Try it for yourself: listen to a recording without the intention of answering questions, then compare it to listening with the intent of remembering and understanding. Notice how your listening intensity changes when you're truly focused.

Why We Struggle to Listen

Why is listening challenging for most of us if listening is so important? Several factors contribute to this struggle:

1. *Distractions*: Constant noise from devices, social media, and our own thoughts makes it difficult to focus. Divided attention causes us to lose track of what's being said, signalling to the speaker that they don't have our full attention.

2. *Our Agenda*: We often enter conversations with a preconceived agenda. Instead of truly listening, we focus on what we want to say next. This tunnel vision prevents us from thoroughly engaging and can lead to missed opportunities for understanding.

3. *Impatience*: We live in a world that values speed, quick answers, and fast results. This impatience seeps into our conversations, making us want people to "get to the point" quickly and causing us to overlook important nuances.

4. *Emotional Reactions*: Certain topics or statements can make us defensive, angry, or even embarrassed. Emotional reactions can override our ability to listen objectively, blocking us from fully understanding the other person.

5. *Ego and the Need to Be Right*: Our desire to prove ourselves or be "right" can stifle open communication. Instead of collaborating, we compete, which needs to be changed or prevents genuine understanding.

Missed Opportunities to Listen

Consider Lisa, who comes home after a tough day and vents to her partner, Mark, about an argument with her boss. Mark cuts her off, suggesting she should "just talk to the boss tomorrow and clear things up." Mark believes he's being helpful, but he misses the point. Lisa isn't looking for a solution; she wants to feel heard. We miss opportunities for empathy, connection, and support when we fail to listen.

Reflect on a time when you offered advice instead of empathy. What might have been different if you had simply listened?

How to Become a Better Listener

The good news is that listening is a skill that can be developed with practice. Here are practical steps to help you become a better listener:

1. *Be Present*: Give your undivided attention to the speaker. Put away distractions like your phone and make eye contact to show engagement. Presence communicates respect and value to the speaker.

2. *Practice Active Listening*: Engage with the speaker by asking clarifying questions and paraphrasing. For example, if someone says, "I've been feeling overwhelmed at work, "you might respond, "It sounds like you have had a lot on your plate. What's been the most challenging part?"

3. *Avoid Interrupting*: Allow the speaker to finish before responding. Letting someone speak without interruption provides a space where they feel truly heard.

4. *Mirror Emotions, Not Just Words*: Reflect the speaker's emotions to show empathy. Instead of saying, "I understand," try, "It sounds like this has been tough for you."

5. *Practice Silence*: Allow the speaker time to express themselves without interruption. Silence can be powerful, especially when discussing sensitive topics.

6. *Show Understanding through Body Language*: Maintain eye contact, use open gestures, and align your body language

with the tone of the conversation to reinforce your attentiveness.

7. *Clarify and Summarise*: Summarise or paraphrase the speaker's words to ensure both parties agree and prevent misunderstandings.

8. *Listen Without Judgement*: Approach conversations with an open mind. Set aside biases and focus on understanding the speaker's perspective.

Different Listening Styles

1. *Passive Listening*: Hearing without engaging, often when tired or uninterested.

2. *Selective Listening*: Focusing only on parts that interest us, leading to misunderstandings.

3. *Active Listening*: Engaging fully with the speaker, providing feedback, and seeking to understand the message.

4. *Empathetic Listening*: Listening to understand the speaker's emotions, fostering trust and connection.

5. *Relationship Listening*: Listening because the relationship matters, not necessarily the content.

6. *Critical Listening*: Evaluating or analysing information, particularly in professional settings.

7. *Non-judgmental Listening*: Listening without forming judgments fosters open dialogue.

Empathetic Listening and Relationship Listening have profoundly impacted my personal and professional life. Let me illustrate:

Suppose you have a five-year-old relative named Veda who's in tears over losing her favourite doll. How would you respond? Perhaps you'd offer to search for the doll, buy a new one, or distract her with a treat. But would you also consider simply holding her hand, listening, and letting her know you understand her sadness?

Empathetic listeners provide emotional support, not just solutions. They create a space where people feel genuinely understood. Where in your life could you benefit from listening more empathetically?

I remember how my young son would excitedly share every detail of his day with me, even when I came exhausted from college. While his stories may have seemed trivial in the grander scheme of things, they were his whole world at that moment. Listening to him with genuine attention and the same energy he had wasn't about the content; it was about showing him that he mattered and that his voice was valued. These small, intentional acts of connection reinforced our relationship and taught me that meaningful communication is often about presence, not just words. These evenings have strengthened our bond with each other.

We need to learn to listen to people not because they make sense to us every time but because they matter; our relationship with them matters to us, be it in our personal or professional lives. Reflect and make a list of the people in your life whom you should listen to more attentively because they truly matter!

The Benefits of Effective Listening

1. *Strengthening Trust*: Genuine listening builds trust. When someone feels truly heard, they're more likely to open up.

2. *Improving Emotional Intelligence*: Listening helps us recognise and respond to others' emotions, improving both personal and professional relationships.

3. *Enhancing problem-solving abilities*: Effective listening allows us to gather all the puzzle pieces, leading to better, informed solutions.

4. *The Ripple Effect:* Effective listening improves interactions across all aspects of life, creating a more supportive environment where everyone feels valued.

5. *Reducing Conflicts:* Listening can prevent misunderstandings and help de, de-escalate conflicts by clarifying differing perspectives.

Imagine a manager who often dominates team meetings. After practising active listening, they listen with an open mind, leading to increased team morale, better collaboration, and even more innovative ideas. By mastering the art of listening, this manager transforms their communication and the team's dynamics.

Listening as a Transformative Skill

Listening is more than just a passive act; it's a transformative skill that can change your relationships, work, and life. By being present, practising active listening, and approaching conversations with empathy, you can create stronger connections and more meaningful interactions. The next time you're in a conversation, try something different: pause, listen, and genuinely try to understand the person in front of you. You'll be surprised by the difference it makes.

Summary

In this chapter, we've explored listening as an essential yet often overlooked communication skill. Drawing from Stephen R. Covey's quote, "Most people do not listen with the intent to understand; they listen with the intent to reply," we've highlighted the difference between hearing and listening. Authentic listening requires focus, empathy, and presence, which are rare in today's fast-paced world.

We discussed the barriers to effective listening, such as distractions, impatience, and ego. We also discussed empathetic listening, a style that fosters deeper connection and provides practical steps for becoming a better listener. These practices can transform your personal and professional relationships, fostering trust, empathy, and effective communication.

Key Takeaways

1. **Listening vs. Hearing**: Hearing is passive; listening is active and involves understanding meaning and emotions.

2. **Barriers to Listening**: Distractions, impatience, emotional reactions, and ego are common obstacles.

3. **Empathetic and Non-judgmental Listening**: These types require focusing on the speaker's emotions without judgment.

4. **Practical Tips for Better Listening**:
   - Be present: Remove distractions.
   - Practice active listening: Engage and paraphrase.
   - Avoid interrupting: Let the speaker finish.
   - Mirror emotions: Show empathy.
   - Listen without judgement: Approach conversations with openness.

5. **Benefits of Listening**: Effective listening strengthens relationships, builds trust, reduces conflicts, and positively impacts communication.

Reflection Activity

1. Reflect on a Time You Felt Unheard: How would the conversation have changed if the other person had practised empathetic listening?

2. Ego and Emotional Reactions: Consider when your ego or emotions interfere with listening. What can you do differently next time?

Self-Assessment Checklist

Evaluate your listening habits on a scale from 0 (Not at all) to 5 (All the time):

1. I give my full attention during conversations. ___ / 5

2. I actively engage by asking clarifying questions. ___ / 5

3. I avoid interrupting and wait for the speaker to finish. ___ / 5

4. I try to understand the emotions behind the speaker's words. ___ / 5

5. I practise empathetic and non-judgmental listening to build stronger connections. ___ / 5

Chapter 4

THE POWER OF QUESTIONS: UNLOCKING CLARITY AND INTENT IN COMMUNICATION

"Good communication is the bridge between confusion and clarity."

—Nat Turner

Communication is more than just the exchange of words; it is the cornerstone of understanding, trust, and growth. As Nat Turner aptly puts it, transparent communication bridges confusion and clarity, and questions are the bricks that build this bridge. Questions are not merely tools to seek information but catalysts for reflection, deeper understanding, and connection.

Research by Harvard Business Review has shown that asking thoughtful questions fosters trust, encourages collaboration, and deepens engagement in both personal and professional settings. For instance, in a study by Harvard researchers, leaders who asked more questions and sought input from their teams were rated more approachable and practical, ultimately achieving higher team productivity and morale.

Consider a manager overseeing a project that's running behind schedule. Instead of expressing frustration or giving orders, the manager pauses and asks, "What challenges are you facing that we can address together?" This single question shifts the conversation from blame to problem-solving, encouraging the team to open up about roadblocks and collaborate on solutions.

This example leads us to explore the critical elements of communication: questions, clarity, and intention. Each element holds immense potential on its own, but when merged, it creates a transformative impact on communication. Let us first explore the role of questions in effective communication.

The Power of Questions

Questions are far more than tools for gathering information they are the keys to unlocking curiosity, deepening relationships, and fostering meaningful dialogue. When wielded effectively, questions catalyse understanding, clarity, and growth. As Warren Berger eloquently argues in *A More Beautiful Question*, asking the right questions can challenge assumptions, ignite innovation, and lead to transformational insights.

Why Questions Matter in Communication

Questions have the unique ability to shift a conversation from transactional to transformational. They open the door to exploration, inviting deeper understanding and connection. In professional settings, they stimulate collaboration and problem-solving. In personal relationships, they foster empathy and emotional connection. By asking thoughtful questions, we seek answers and create a space for others to feel heard and valued.

Consider this: A leader who asks their team, "What can we do differently to make this process smoother for everyone?" is not just seeking feedback. They're empowering their team, encouraging creativity, and demonstrating that their perspectives matter. This single question can elevate team morale and productivity far beyond what a directive statement could achieve.

Types of Questions and Their Impact

1. **Open-ended Questions**: They invite exploration and encourage expansive responses, fostering creativity and dialogue.

   - Instead of asking, "Did you like the presentation?" try, "What stood out to you in the presentation, and how could we improve it?"

2. **Clarifying Questions**: These ensure mutual understanding and eliminate ambiguity.

   - "When you say we should focus on quality, do you mean we should allocate more time to refining the final output?"

3. **Empathetic Questions:** These show genuine care and understanding, building trust and connection.

   - "How has this challenge been affecting you, and is there any way I can support you better?"

4. **Probing Questions**: These dig deeper into underlying issues, uncovering root causes or hidden concerns.

   - "What do you think might be causing the delays, and how can we address them together?"

Questions are not just about seeking answers they can resolve conflicts, build bridges, and inspire transformation. For example, when faced with a tense disagreement, asking, "What's most important to you in this situation?" can de-escalate emotions and uncover shared goals, paving the way for resolution.

Think back to when a single question shifted the course of a conversation or opened up a new perspective. Was it a clarifying question that resolved confusion? Or an empathetic question that strengthened a bond? Recognizing the impact of thoughtful questions helps us harness their power more intentionally.

Asking with Purpose

Asking the right questions transforms how we interact with others, allowing us to move beyond surface-level exchanges into profound, meaningful dialogue. Drawing from the insights of thought leaders like Warren Berger, questions serve as tools to unlock human potential, build connections, and foster innovation. The next time you are conversing, pause and ask yourself: *What question could open the door to deeper understanding or inspire new possibilities?*

The Importance of Clarity in Communication

While questions open the door to exploration and understanding, clarity ensures that the message crosses that threshold and lands precisely as intended. Without clarity, even the most well-intentioned questions or conversations risk being misunderstood, leading to confusion, misaligned goals, and lost opportunities.

Why Clarity Matters

Clarity in communication creates a shared understanding. It eliminates ambiguity, aligns expectations, and builds trust. In professional settings, clear communication drives efficiency and prevents errors. In personal relationships, it fosters transparency and deeper connections. As Brené Brown highlights in *Dare to Lead*, clear is kind. While often unintentional, unclear communication can result in frustration or resentment when expectations are not met.

Principles of Clarity

1. **Be Precise:** Precision in language removes the guesswork from communication. Vague statements can leave listeners unsure of what is being asked or expected, while specific language provides actionable guidance.

- Instead of saying, "We should finish this soon," say, "Let's complete this by Thursday at 3 PM." The latter leaves no room for ambiguity and provides a clear timeline for action.

2. **Simplify Complex Ideas**: Simplifying doesn't mean oversimplifying; it means breaking down complex concepts into digestible, relatable terms. Using analogies or examples helps bridge gaps in understanding, especially when addressing diverse audiences with varying levels of expertise.

   - A teacher explaining a complex math concept might say, "Think of it like splitting a pizza evenly among friends." This analogy translates a potentially abstract idea into a tangible, familiar scenario.

3. **Check for Understanding**: Communication doesn't end when the message is delivered it ends when it is understood. Follow-up questions ensure alignment and allow for clarification if needed.

   - After outlining a plan, ask, "Does this make sense? Is there anything you'd like me to explain further?" This practice not only ensures clarity but also demonstrates care and attentiveness.

Elon Musk's Clarity in Leadership

Elon Musk exemplifies the power of clarity in driving ambitious projects. As the CEO of SpaceX, Musk didn't just articulate a dream of colonizing Mars; he laid out detailed plans that transformed his vision into tangible milestones. Musk breaks down monumental goals into smaller, actionable steps in public presentations and team discussions, using clear timelines and technical specifics.

For instance, when introducing the concept of reusable rockets, Musk didn't rely on abstract ideas. He explained the technological hurdles, the economic benefits, and the steps needed to achieve the goal. This clarity inspired confidence among stakeholders, including employees, investors, and even sceptics, enabling SpaceX to achieve unprecedented milestones in aerospace innovation.

Musk's clarity illustrates how effective communication can bridge the gap between vision and reality, creating a sense of shared purpose and direction.

Practical Steps to Communicate with Clarity

1. **Organize Your Thoughts**: Before speaking or writing, outline your main points. Structured thinking ensures a coherent flow of ideas, reducing the risk of confusion.

   - Use the "Rule of Three" to highlight three key ideas to make your message concise and memorable.

2. **Tailor Your Message to Your Audience**: Adjust your language, tone, and examples to match the needs and familiarity of your audience. What works in a professional presentation may not resonate in casual conversations.

   - Focus on specifics and data for a technical audience. For a general audience, prioritize relatable analogies and simpler language.

3. **Use Visual Aids When Necessary**: Charts, diagrams, and other visuals can reinforce your message and help clarify complex ideas.

   - In a meeting about project timelines, a Gantt chart can visually communicate deadlines and dependencies, making the plan easier to understand.

4. **Eliminate Jargon**

   - Industry-specific terms can alienate or confuse people outside your field. Replace jargon with simple, universally understood terms unless your audience shares the same technical expertise.

5. **Reiterate Key Points**: Summarising your main message at the end of a conversation or presentation reinforces understanding.

    *   Conclude a meeting by saying, "To recap, our next steps are [specific actions], and our deadline is [specific date]."

When communication is clear, it empowers both the speaker and the listener. Misunderstandings are minimized, confidence is built, and collaboration becomes seamless. Whether you're leading a team, presenting an idea, or resolving a conflict, clarity transforms interactions into meaningful exchanges of ideas.

As Brené Brown wisely observed, "Clear is kind. Unclear is unkind." Practicing clarity in communication isn't just a skill; it's an act of respect and empathy. By speaking with precision, simplifying complex ideas, and ensuring alignment, we can build bridges of understanding that support collaboration, innovation, and trust.

Speaking with Intention

Intent transforms communication from a mere exchange of words into a purposeful and meaningful connection. It's not just about the message you deliver; it's about understanding *why* you're delivering it and aligning your words with your deeper goals, values, and audience needs. Speaking with intention ensures that your communication inspires trust, fosters understanding, and achieves its desired outcomes.

Why Intention Matters

When communication lacks intention, it risks becoming hollow or misguided, failing to connect with the audience. Intentional communication, conversely, is guided by clarity of purpose and thoughtfulness, making every interaction meaningful. As Simon Sinek emphasises in *Start With Why*, people connect not with *what* you say but with *why* you say it. Intent gives communication its emotional and intellectual resonance, creating a lasting impact.

Key Elements of Intentional Communication

1. **Understand Your Goal**: Every intentional communication starts with a clear goal. Identifying why you are speaking ensures that your words align with your purpose.

   Before a meeting, a manager decides their goal is to motivate employees for an upcoming project. Instead of delivering technical details first, they lead with an inspiring story about overcoming challenges, setting a tone of enthusiasm and optimism.

2. **Tailor Your Message to the Audience**: Effective communication considers the audience's needs, preferences, and contexts. Intention requires adapting tone, language, and delivery based on who you're addressing.

   Consider Martin Luther King Jr.'s *"I Have a Dream"* speech. King tailored his words to resonate with both oppressed individuals seeking hope and allies seeking understanding. His intentional use of universal values like freedom and equality ensured his message transcended racial and cultural boundaries.

3. **Align Words with Actions**: Consistency is a cornerstone of intentional communication. When your words and actions align, they reinforce trust and credibility. Misalignment, on the other hand, breeds doubt and diminishes influence.

   A teacher who tells students the value of punctuality must model it by arriving on time for class. This consistency reinforces their message, making it credible and respected.

4. **Deliver with Authenticity:** Authentic communication stems from a genuine belief in your message. It's about being true to your values while connecting with others.

Brené Brown's *Dare to Lead* highlights that vulnerability and authenticity are essential for intentional communication. Speaking with courage and honesty allows leaders to connect on a human level, inspiring loyalty and collaboration.

Oprah Winfrey is a master of intentional communication, blending purpose and authenticity to create meaningful dialogue. Whether interviewing a celebrity, discussing societal issues, or addressing her audience, Oprah tailors her message to resonate deeply. Her ability to connect stems from aligning her words with her empathy, empowerment, and understanding core values.

Speaking with intention transforms communication from a transaction into a connection. It ensures that every word, tone, and gesture is aligned with purpose, building trust, fostering understanding, and inspiring action. By infusing clarity and intention into your communication, you create effective exchanges and meaningful relationships that leave a lasting impact.

The Synergy of Questions, Clarity, and Intention

When questions, clarity, and intention come together, they form a powerful trifecta that elevates communication from mere exchanges to transformative experiences. Each element serves a distinct purpose. Questions open the door to exploration, clarity ensures the message is understood, and intention provides the purpose and emotional resonance. Together, they create a communication style that is both impactful and meaningful.

Imagine a manager addressing a team struggling to meet a project deadline. The conversation begins collaboratively if the manager asks, "What challenges are we facing, and how can I support you?" (Question). He ensures everyone is aligned on the next steps by following up with, "Let's prioritise these three tasks by Friday at noon to stay on track" (Clarity). Finally, the manager conveys confidence and motivation by expressing, "I trust in your abilities, and together, we can achieve this" (Intention).

This synergy builds trust, inspires collaboration, and drives results. Here's a deeper look at how these elements interact:

1. Questions: Opening the Pathway to Understanding

Questions initiate the flow of dialogue, inviting others to share perspectives and contribute ideas. They are willing to listen and learn, laying the groundwork for authentic connection.

In a classroom, a teacher struggling to engage students might ask, "What topics excite you the most, and how can we incorporate those into our lessons?" This question transforms the dynamic, showing students that their input matters and encouraging active participation.

Impact: Questions create openness, foster trust, and allow communication to adapt to the moment's needs.

2. Clarity: Eliminating Ambiguity for Effective Action

While questions gather insights, clarity ensures those insights are transformed into actionable steps. Clear communication removes guesswork, reduces confusion, and aligns everyone toward a common goal.

A CEO launching a new initiative might say, "Our goal is to improve customer satisfaction by 15% over the next quarter. Here are three specific actions each team can take to achieve this." The message's precision leaves no room for ambiguity and sets clear expectations.

Impact: Clarity empowers action by aligning intentions with execution, minimizing errors, and building confidence in the speaker's direction.

3. Intention: Adding Purpose and Meaning

While questions and clarity focus on communication structure, intention gives it heart. It reflects the "why" behind the message, ensuring it resonates emotionally and aligns with shared values.

A community leader addressing a town hall might say, "Our goal in revitalizing this park isn't just about aesthetics; it's about creating a space where families can connect and children can thrive." This intentional message inspires commitment by connecting with the audience's deeper values.

Impact: Intention ensures the message transcends information, creating an emotional connection that fosters engagement and trust.

Transforming Communication through Synergy

The true power of communication lies in its ability to connect, inspire, and transform. Questions spark curiosity and engagement; clarity eliminates barriers to understanding; and intention creates emotional resonance and purpose. Together, these elements form a dynamic framework for communication that doesn't just convey information but fosters connection and drives meaningful change.

The next time you engage in a conversation, consider how you can bring these three elements into harmony: ask thoughtful questions, communicate clearly, and speak with purpose. In doing so, you'll elevate your communication and create lasting, positive impacts in your personal and professional relationships.

Summary

The chapter explores the transformative power of combining questions, clarity, and intention to elevate communication. Questions encourage exploration and foster dialogue, clarity ensures understanding and eliminates ambiguity, and intention aligns communication with purpose, building trust and resonance. They create a dynamic synergy that bridges gaps, inspires collaboration, and fosters meaningful connections.

Key Takeaways

1. **Questions Spark Exploration:** Thoughtful questions open the door to deeper understanding and connection, empowering collaboration and fostering creativity.

2. **Clarity Eliminates Ambiguity:** Precision, simplicity, and structured communication ensure messages are understood as intended, aligning expectations and actions.

3. **Intention Aligns Purpose:** Communicating with purpose and authenticity builds trust, enhances emotional resonance, and strengthens relationships.

4. **The Synergy Creates Impact:** Merging questions, clarity, and intention transforms communication into a tool for connection, trust, and innovation.

5. **Practical Application is Key:** Preparing purposeful questions, crafting clear messages, and infusing intention into every interaction ensures lasting success.

Reflection Activity

1. Reflect on a recent conversation where your question shifted the dialogue. How did it change the outcome?

2. Think of a time when unclear communication caused confusion. How could clarity have improved the situation?

3. Recall a moment when your intentions weren't aligned with your words. How did it affect the conversation, and what can you learn from it?

4. Identify a situation where combining thoughtful questions, clear communication, and intentionality led to a positive outcome.

5. Journal your thoughts on how you can integrate these three elements into your daily communication practices.

Self-Assessment Checklist

Rate yourself from 0 (Rarely) to 5 (Consistently):

1. I ask purposeful questions that foster understanding and engagement. ___ / 5

2. I communicate clearly, eliminating ambiguity and aligning expectations. ___ / 5

3. I ensure my words, tone, and body language align with my intentions. ___ / 5

4. I actively listen to responses, validating others' perspectives. ___ / 5

5. I use the synergy of questions, clarity, and intention to enhance my communication. ___ / 5

Part 1: Foundations of Communication, Situational Skill Building

Instructions: Review each scenario and consider how you would apply the skills and insights from Part 1. Feel free to use the empty space to jot down your reflection!

- *A family member is upset, but they aren't saying much. You want to support them without prying. How would you use Non-verbal cues and empathetic listening to create a safe space for them to open up?*

- *During a team meeting, you're asked for input on an unfamiliar project. How would you handle this situation, using self-awareness to communicate clearly without undermining your confidence?*

- *A close friend is talking to you about a significant decision they're struggling with, and they're looking for advice. How can you practice reflective listening to help them feel understood and supported without offering unsolicited advice?*

- *You're explaining a project process to a new colleague, but they seem confused. Considering your tone, pacing, and approach, how would you adjust your communication to ensure they understand?*

- *During a conversation with a friend, you notice they aren't fully engaged. Instead of feeling slighted, how could you interpret their body language and adjust your approach to re-engage them or check if something else is on their mind?*

- *You're presenting an idea in a meeting, and someone immediately questions your approach. How can you use active listening to understand their perspective, summarize their concerns, and keep the discussion constructive?*

PART 2

TRANSFORMING HOW YOU COMMUNICATE WITH OTHERS

"To effectively communicate, we must realize that we are all different in the way we perceive the world and use this understanding as a guide to our communication with others."

— Tony Robbins

With the foundational principles in place, it's time to delve into the transformative art of connecting with others. Communication is more than exchanging words; it's about understanding perspectives, fostering trust, and creating shared meaning. Part 2 is your guide to communicating with clarity, intention, and empathy, whether addressing a loved one, collaborating with a colleague, or navigating a challenging discussion.

This section provides tools to help you speak with purpose, navigate conflicts gracefully, and harness the subtle power of Non-verbal communication. Imagine approaching any conversation comforting a friend in distress or presenting a bold idea at work with the confidence and skill to connect deeply and leave a lasting impact.

As you journey through these chapters, you'll learn to move beyond self-expression to communication that inspires action, collaboration, and understanding. These lessons will teach you how to bridge differences, encourage shared goals, and transform everyday conversations into opportunities for positive change.

Each chapter invites you to explore the art of intentional dialogue, helping you embrace communication's transformative potential in your personal and professional relationships. In this context, communication becomes a catalyst for growth and meaningful connection.

Chapter 5

WHAT AFFECTS COMMUNICATION THE MOST? BARRIERS AND NAVIGATING DIFFICULT CONVERSATIONS

"The single biggest problem in communication is the illusion that it has taken place."

—George Bernard Shaw

Imagine carefully crafting a heartfelt message, only to realize later that the other person completely misunderstood your intent. You walk away wondering, "How could they misinterpret me so entirely?" This gap between what we say and what others hear is surprisingly common, often fuelled by unseen barriers like assumptions, past experiences, and emotional states. These hidden obstacles can cloud our words and distort our intentions, making meaningful connections challenging.

In this chapter, we'll explore the factors that most impact our communication and identify common barriers that interfere with clarity. You'll learn strategies for navigating difficult conversations with confidence and respect. As you read, think back to times when conversations didn't go as planned and consider the barriers that might have been at play. Equipped with new insights, you'll be ready to approach future interactions with greater empathy and understanding.

Understanding Barriers to Effective Communication

Barriers to communication aren't always obvious; they're often subtle, like unconscious biases, or deeply rooted, like personal fears. These unseen obstacles can colour our words and influence our understanding without realising it. Research by Albert Mehrabian, a pioneer in nonverbal communication, showed that misunderstandings frequently arise from these subtle cues and biases, often leaving both sides feeling unheard. Whether they're right in front of us or hidden in the background, these barriers hold us back from creating clear, productive dialogue. Recognizing and addressing them is essential to fostering genuine, open communication.

Common Barriers to Communication

Physical Barriers

Physical barriers in communication refer to environmental and bodily factors that disrupt our ability to connect and communicate effectively. These barriers can be external, like environmental noise or equipment malfunctions, or internal, such as physical ailments. Though often overlooked, physical barriers play a significant role in limiting clarity, focus, and engagement during interactions.

Environmental Disruptions

Physical barriers can arise from various environmental factors, each of which has the potential to impact how we communicate and understand each other. These disruptions may seem minor but can drastically alter the quality of communication when they go unaddressed.

- **Noise during a Meeting**: Imagine participating in a virtual meeting with colleagues, where everyone is trying to discuss a project deadline. Suddenly, loud construction noises outside your window make it difficult to hear key points or concentrate on what's being said. Background noise like this can fragment a conversation, forcing people to speak louder, repeat themselves, or lose their train of thought.

- **Power Outage during a Presentation**: Picture yourself in the middle of presenting a well-prepared PowerPoint in front of your team. Just as you reach a crucial slide, there's a sudden power outage, cutting off the screen and interrupting the flow of information. This abrupt barrier not only disrupts the visual aids but also forces the presenter to regain focus and adjust the presentation style, often without the supporting materials they'd planned.

- **Temperature Control Issues**: Environmental comfort can play an unexpected role in communication effectiveness. For instance, if you're in a serious, hour-long lecture and the air conditioning malfunctions, the discomfort can easily distract you from concentrating on the content. Minor physical discomforts, like being too warm or cold, can detract from mental engagement and make it difficult to absorb information or interact meaningfully.

Physical Discomfort and Health Barriers

Physical barriers aren't limited to the external environment; internal physical states can also impede communication. When our bodies are in distress, our ability to concentrate, listen actively, and respond appropriately is naturally compromised.

- **Ailments and Illness**: If you're dealing with a headache or fever while trying to focus on work, the discomfort can make it challenging to engage fully. For instance, imagine a scenario where you're in a vital team discussion, but a persistent headache distracts you from catching every detail. You may unintentionally miss out on crucial points or find it challenging to respond thoughtfully because you focus on the conversation and discomfort.

- **Physical Ailments Impacting Responsiveness**: Chronic conditions, such as back pain or fatigue, can also hinder engagement in professional settings. If someone sits through a lengthy meeting while dealing with discomfort, their ability to contribute meaningfully may be affected. Physical pain can reduce mental clarity, make active participation difficult, and leave a person more focused on physical relief than on contributing ideas or processing information.

Language and Cultural Barriers

Language and culture are deeply interwoven, shaping how people express ideas, values, and perspectives. Language often reflects cultural norms, beliefs, and societal values, meaning that cultural differences frequently impact how we use language and interpret messages. Language and cultural nuances usually merge when we interact across cultures, creating a complex layer of potential misunderstandings. Because language and culture are so interdependent, it's essential to address both aspects together to understand these communication barriers better.

Language and Jargon

The words we choose, especially when using technical jargon, slang, or culturally specific phrases, can unintentionally create barriers to understanding. When speaking with people from different backgrounds or knowledge levels, adapting language to ensure inclusivity is essential. Clear, simple language allows our message to resonate with a broader audience, making our communication accessible and fostering a welcoming space for meaningful engagement.

Medical Jargon in Patient Communication

Consider a doctor explaining a diagnosis using highly technical medical jargon to a patient with limited medical knowledge. The patient may leave feeling more confused than informed, unable to fully comprehend their health situation. However, by simplifying the explanation by using analogies or everyday terms, the doctor can empower the patient to understand their condition and feel comfortable asking questions. This adjustment builds trust and ensures a shared understanding, enhancing the quality of the interaction.

Business Communication across Knowledge Levels

In corporate settings, professionals often use industry-specific terminology. Imagine a financial analyst presenting a report to a diverse team, including finance experts and marketing professionals. If the analyst uses technical, financial terms without explanation, the non-finance team members may feel alienated or miss the key points. However, by explaining complex terms or presenting concepts in simpler language, the analyst can make the information accessible to the team, ensuring everyone remains engaged and informed.

Beyond jargon and vocabulary, other nuances of language, such as accents, gestures, and tone, can also create communication challenges, especially in multicultural environments. For instance, a simple hand gesture like the "OK" sign may signal approval in one culture but be offensive in another. Similarly, accents and dialects influence pronunciation and can affect how messages are perceived, as seen in India, where regional variations in English can subtly impact understanding. Even tone and formality carry significant weight; in some settings, a formal tone conveys respect, while in others, it may appear distant or impersonal. Recognizing these subtleties allows for a more inclusive approach to communication, reducing misunderstandings and fostering mutual respect across diverse backgrounds.

Cultural Differences

Cultural norms shape how people express themselves, listen, and interpret messages. Unaware of these differences, misunderstandings can arise from varied customs, values, and expectations. For example, while direct eye contact may be seen as a sign of confidence in some cultures, it may be perceived as disrespectful or aggressive in others. Similarly, in cultures that value indirect communication, people may rely more on context and nonverbal cues than on explicit words, creating confusion for those accustomed to a more direct style.

Being culturally sensitive means paying attention to nonverbal cues, conversational styles, and greeting norms that may differ from our own. Cultivating this awareness fosters more inclusive and respectful communication, bridging gaps between diverse perspectives.

Eye Contact in Cross-Cultural Business Settings

Consider a scenario where an American business professional meets with a Japanese colleague. In American culture, maintaining eye contact is seen as a sign of attentiveness and honesty, but in Japanese culture, prolonged eye contact can be considered impolite. The American professional's direct gaze might make the Japanese colleague uncomfortable, affecting their willingness to share openly. Understanding this difference, the American professional could adjust their approach, focusing more on tone and verbal cues to convey engagement while respecting the Japanese colleague's cultural norms.

Hierarchical Language in Multinational Teams

In multinational teams, cultural differences in language reflect varying attitudes toward hierarchy and authority. In some cultures, people are encouraged to address superiors directly and casually, while formal titles and respectful language are essential in others. For instance, a German team member addressing their superiors by first name might be overly casual or disrespectful to a Japanese colleague, who might be accustomed to a more formal hierarchy. This difference could lead to misunderstandings or perceived disrespect if team members aren't aware of each other's cultural backgrounds.

Reference for Deeper Insight

In *The Culture Map: Breaking Through the Invisible Boundaries of Global Business*, Erin Meyer explores how cultural differences affect communication in international teams. Meyer emphasizes that cultural variations in language, hierarchy, and feedback styles often create barriers to clear understanding. Her work provides a framework for understanding these differences and navigating cultural nuances in communication, making it an invaluable resource for anyone working across diverse backgrounds.

Multilingual Communication in Indian Workplaces

In India, a country known for its linguistic diversity, people speak over 20 officially recognized languages, with hundreds of regional dialects. Imagine a workplace in Mumbai where team members come from various parts of India each bringing their regional language, cultural norms, and communication styles. In a team meeting, some employees may speak primarily in Hindi, while others may be more comfortable with English or a regional language like Marathi, Telugu, or Tamil.

During discussions, certain employees may naturally switch to their native language when talking with colleagues from the same region. While this may feel comfortable for them, it can unintentionally exclude others who don't speak that language. Additionally, gestures and expressions can carry different meanings across regions. For instance, a head bobble that signifies agreement in South India might be confusing to someone from another region unfamiliar with the gesture.

Impact on Communication

This linguistic and cultural diversity creates both opportunities and challenges. Without a common language or an awareness of regional differences, team members may misinterpret each other's gestures or feel excluded from conversations. However, the organization can bridge these gaps by establishing a language policy (such as using English for all formal communication) and fostering a culturally inclusive environment. Encouraging employees to learn basic greetings or expressions from each other's languages can also build camaraderie and mutual respect.

Lesson

This scenario highlights how a multicultural society like India, with its rich tapestry of languages and customs, requires intentional inclusivity in communication. Recognizing these regional variations and fostering a shared understanding can help create a more cohesive and collaborative workplace where everyone feels valued and understood.

Psychological Barriers

Psychological barriers in communication refer to the internal mental and emotional states that shape how we perceive, process, and respond to information. These barriers often stem from assumptions, biases, emotions, or previous experiences, all of which influence how we interpret messages and engage with others. In *The Seven Principles for Making Marriage Work*, Dr. John Gottman discusses the impact of "emotional filters" in relationships, which affect not only our ability to communicate effectively but also our capacity to empathize and connect. Understanding these psychological filters, or barriers, is crucial for developing meaningful and constructive communication.

Assumptions and Preconceptions

Assumptions arise when we expect others to share our perspectives or interpret things as we do. Preconceptions, conversely, involve preconceived ideas about how someone will respond, which may or may not align with reality. Both assumptions and preconceptions can cloud our communication, as they create a gap between what we intend to convey and what is understood.

Imagine a manager who assumes their team fully understands the goals of a project simply because they mentioned it once in a meeting. The manager doesn't clarify further, assuming the team is on the same page. Later, frustration and confusion arise when the team's work doesn't align with the manager's vision. This situation highlights how unchecked assumptions can lead to misalignment, potentially impacting morale and productivity.

In my life, I once held unspoken expectations of my loved ones, assuming they would automatically understand my needs. When they acted differently from what I had anticipated, I often felt disappointed or resentful while they remained completely unaware of my expectations. Over time, I learned that these assumptions, rather than their actions, were the source of my frustration. By expressing my needs openly, I was able to build stronger, more understanding relationships, free from the misunderstandings that had previously caused tension.

Emotional Influences

Emotions play an influential role in communication. When we're stressed, anxious, or frustrated, our words and tone may unintentionally reflect those feelings, impacting the clarity and reception of our message. High emotions can cloud judgment, making it challenging to listen actively or respond constructively.

Emotional Influences in Customer Service

Consider a customer service representative who had difficulty interacting with a frustrated customer. Still feeling the residual tension, they move on to the next call but find it challenging to mask their frustration. The unintended sharpness in their tone affects how the new customer perceives the interaction, leading to a less satisfactory exchange. This example shows how emotional states, if unchecked, can carry over and negatively influence subsequent interactions, regardless of the new person's demeanour.

In personal relationships, heightened emotions during arguments can lead to impulsive, hurtful comments. When emotions like anger or frustration take control, it's easy to lose sight of the conversation's purpose and focus instead on venting them. Recognizing one's emotional state and pausing can be a powerful way to reduce miscommunication in these instances.

Personal Bias and Stereotypes

Our conscious or unconscious biases shape how we perceive others and interpret their messages. These biases are often based on stereotypes, past experiences, or cultural influences, leading us to make snap judgments or assumptions about someone's intentions. Recognizing our biases is critical to approaching conversations more openly and objectively.

Biases in Hiring Decisions

Imagine a hiring manager who unconsciously favours candidates from a specific educational background, believing they're inherently more qualified. This bias may prevent the manager from recognizing candidates' skills with alternative experiences, leading to missed opportunities for diverse talent. By becoming aware of their biases, the manager could approach interviews more objectively, focusing on relevant skills rather than preconceived notions.

Biases can affect how we interpret feedback from others in daily interactions. For example, if a person believes that their colleague is overly critical, they may view any constructive feedback from that colleague as negative, regardless of the content. This psychological barrier distorts the message and limits opportunities for growth and improvement.

Gender Biases in Communication

Gender biases subtly influence how we communicate and interpret messages. In *You Just Don't Understand: Women and Men in Conversation*, linguist Deborah Tannen explores how men and women often adopt different conversational styles. For instance, women may focus on building rapport and empathy, while men may prioritize assertiveness and problem-solving. These differing styles can lead to misinterpretations, especially in settings where gender roles are deeply ingrained or expected.

Gender Bias in Workplace Meetings

Women's contributions are often interrupted in meetings more frequently than men's. Research shows that these interruptions can discourage women from fully participating, leading to a loss of valuable input. In contrast, men may feel societal pressure to communicate assertively, even when a collaborative approach would be more effective. Recognizing these biases and adjusting communication styles can create a more inclusive and respectful environment, encouraging open dialogue across genders.

Gender biases can also impact how feedback is received. A woman who communicates assertively may be seen as "bossy" or "overly ambitious," while an empathetic male communicator may be viewed as "soft." These stereotypes can hinder genuine understanding and create unnecessary barriers to effective communication.

When it comes to discussing the barriers to communication, there's no end to the examples, explanations, case studies, or my experiences. One needs to be vigilant while communicating in every situation to overcome these barriers and master the art of communication.

Navigating Difficult Conversations

Difficult conversations are a natural part of life in professional settings or personal relationships. These discussions often involve complex emotions and high stakes, becoming defensive or avoidant quickly. However, research shows that when approached with empathy, assertiveness, and emotional regulation, challenging conversations can strengthen relationships and foster growth. In *Crucial Conversations: Tools for Talking When Stakes Are High*, the authors explore how mastering these discussions can lead to powerful breakthroughs in understanding. Here's how to navigate difficult conversations with a balance of empathy, assertiveness, and tact.

Prepare Mentally and Emotionally

Before entering a difficult conversation, take a moment to centre yourself. Reflect on your goals and intentions: What do you hope to achieve, and what emotions are you bringing into the discussion? Being clear on your objectives helps prevent misunderstandings and enables you to approach the conversation calmly and purposefully.

If you need to discuss an issue with a colleague, clarify your goals beforehand. Are you seeking a resolution, an apology, or simply a chance to express your perspective? Knowing your objectives can guide the tone and direction of your approach, helping you remain focused and respectful.

Listen Actively and Validate the Other Person's Perspective

Active listening is a cornerstone of effective communication, especially in challenging conversations. Giving the other person your full attention, showing empathy, and validating their feelings fosters a respectful environment. Research suggests that validation helps reduce defensiveness, as people feel more understood and valued.

In a workplace setting, you might say, "I hear that you're concerned about the changes, and I understand that they impact your workflow. Let's discuss how we can make this transition smoother for you." Even if you disagree, acknowledging their viewpoint shows that you are committed to understanding, which can make finding a solution easier.

Express Yourself Clearly and Assertively

When communicating your viewpoint, strive for clarity and assertiveness. Avoid passive or aggressive language, focusing on respectful, direct statements. "I" statements, such as "I feel" or "I need," keep the focus on your perspective and help prevent the other person from feeling blamed.

Instead of saying, "You always interrupt me," try, "I feel unheard when I'm interrupted, and I'd appreciate a chance to finish my thoughts." This approach communicates your feelings assertively while keeping the tone respectful.

Stay Open to Compromise

Being flexible and open to alternative solutions is crucial for collaboration in difficult conversations. Compromise doesn't mean sacrificing your needs; it's about finding common ground that respects both parties' perspectives.

If a project deadline is causing tension with a team member, consider options together. You might say, "Would it help if we re-prioritized tasks or set smaller, achievable goals along the way?" This willingness to adapt can ease tensions and create a path that works for everyone.

Manage Your Emotions and Stay Calm

Strong emotions can quickly escalate a difficult conversation. Practicing mindfulness techniques, like deep breathing or briefly pausing, can help maintain composure. Studies show that emotional regulation can reduce impulsivity and keep discussions constructive, even when topics are sensitive.

If you feel anger rising during a conversation, pause, take a deep breath, and refocus. If you need to gather yourself, say, "Let me take a moment to collect my thoughts." This simple pause can prevent the conversation from devolving into conflict and ensure a more productive exchange.

Follow Up if Needed

Following up after a challenging conversation reinforces understanding and shows commitment to resolving any remaining issues. A simple check-in message or conversation can ensure that both parties are on the same page, demonstrating respect and dedication to building trust.

"Thanks for taking the time to talk. I just wanted to check in and see how you feel about our discussion." This follow-up invites further dialogue and strengthens the relationship by showing that the conversation's impact goes beyond the initial interaction.

Practical Strategies for Reducing Barriers in Everyday Communication

Improving communication requires actively reducing barriers. Here are practical steps to enhance daily interactions' clarity, connection, and understanding.

Cultivate Self-Awareness

Self-awareness is essential for identifying and addressing communication tendencies and biases. Regular reflection on your communication habits helps you recognize patterns, such as interrupting or assuming others understand you. Awareness enables you to make conscious changes that improve your interactions.

Reflect on a recent conversation where you may have interrupted. Ask yourself why it happened and consider how you could handle similar situations more thoughtfully.

Practice Mindful Communication

Mindfulness in communication involves fully engaging in the moment without distractions. Maintaining eye contact, giving your full attention, and being present in the conversation reduce misunderstandings and demonstrate respect for the other person's perspective.

During a discussion, put away devices and focus entirely on the conversation. This presence signals respect and fosters a more meaningful exchange.

Ask Open-Ended Questions

Open-ended questions encourage others to share their thoughts and feelings openly, creating space for mutual understanding. These questions are helpful in conversations where assumptions or biases may exist.

Instead of asking, "Did you understand the instructions?" try, "How do you feel about our approach?" This phrasing invites a more profound response, allowing you to gauge the other person's feelings and insights more accurately.

Adjust Your Language and Tone

Using clear, inclusive language minimizes confusion. Avoid jargon and adapt your language to the other person's knowledge level. Tone also plays a significant role in how your message is received, as it can convey respect, empathy, or even unintended frustration.

When explaining a concept to someone unfamiliar with the topic, use straightforward language and periodically check in with questions like, "Does this make sense so far?" This approach ensures the other person feels included and engaged.

Seek Feedback

Feedback from others is a valuable tool for improving communication. Asking for honest input helps you identify areas where barriers may arise, showing that you value their perspective and are committed to growth.

After a presentation, you could ask a colleague, "Was my explanation clear? Is there anything I could improve?" This openness to feedback creates a learning opportunity and fosters stronger, more transparent communication habits.

Reflecting on Communication Habits

Improving communication is a lifelong journey that benefits from ongoing self-reflection and intentional practice. To better understand your communication barriers, consider the following questions:

- **Are specific assumptions or biases influencing how I perceive others' messages?**
- **Do I often feel misunderstood in certain settings? If so, what patterns can I identify?**
- **How do my emotions affect my ability to listen and respond thoughtfully?**

Understanding and addressing these barriers requires a conscious effort, but the reward is a foundation for open, respectful, and meaningful connections with others. Difficult conversations are inevitable, but by cultivating self-awareness, practicing active listening, and approaching discussions with empathy, we can transform these interactions into opportunities for growth and understanding.

Summary

This chapter explored strategies for navigating difficult conversations and overcoming communication barriers, emphasizing empathy, assertiveness, and mindfulness. It began by addressing the challenges of tough discussions, often involving complex emotions and high stakes. Readers were guided through essential techniques, such as preparing mentally, practicing active listening, expressing oneself assertively, staying open to compromise, managing emotions, and following up when necessary.

The chapter also highlighted practical approaches to reducing communication barriers in daily interactions, including cultivating self-awareness, practicing mindful presence, asking open-ended questions, adjusting language and tone, and seeking feedback. Readers were encouraged to reflect on their communication habits, identifying personal biases, assumptions, and emotional influences that could impact their interactions. By recognizing and actively addressing these barriers, readers could lay the foundation for more open, respectful, and meaningful connections, transforming even the most challenging conversations into opportunities for personal growth and stronger relationships.

Key Takeaways

- **Recognize Common Barriers**: Identifying assumptions, biases, emotional influences, and other obstacles helps prevent misunderstandings and fosters clearer communication.

- **Practice Active Listening**: Giving full attention and validating others' perspectives builds trust and respect, laying the groundwork for open dialogue.

- **Use "I" Statements for Clarity**: Expressing yourself assertively with "I" statements, rather than assigning blame, encourages honest and constructive conversation.

- **Stay Calm and Composed**: Managing emotions, especially in challenging discussions, keeps the focus on finding solutions rather than escalating conflict.

- **Follow up to Reinforce Understanding**: Checking in after difficult conversations enhances mutual understanding and shows commitment to growth and respect.

Reflection Activity

Reflect on your communication style by considering the following questions:

1. What barriers do I commonly face in conversations, and what steps can I take to address them?

2. How do I ensure I'm assertive and empathetic in challenging conversations?

3. How can I make active listening a consistent part of my communication approach?

Working through communication barriers and embracing these practices can lead to more fulfilling and respectful interactions.

Every conversation, whether easy or difficult, offers an opportunity to grow and refine communication skills.

Self-Assessment Checklist

Rate each from 0 (Rarely) to 5 (Consistently):

1. I recognize and address common communication barriers when interacting with others. ___ / 5

2. I approach difficult conversations with a calm, solution-oriented mindset. ___ / 5

3. I practice empathy by actively listening to others' perspectives, especially in challenging discussions. ___ / 5

4. I communicate my thoughts and needs clearly, even in high-pressure situations. ___ / 5

5. I respect and acknowledge differing viewpoints, aiming to build mutual understanding. ___ / 5

Chapter 6

ADAPTIVE COMMUNICATION: SHIFTING STYLES BASED ON CONTEXT AND PERSONALITY

"The art of communication is the language of leadership."

—James Humes.

Imagine you're at a dinner gathering with close friends. The conversation flows naturally, filled with laughter and shared stories. Now, picture stepping into a formal work meeting the following day, where your communication style shifts entirely more focused, professional, and concise. Our ability to adapt our communication style based on context and the personalities around us makes interactions effective and impactful. This flexibility reflects our emotional intelligence and demonstrates respect for diverse perspectives, roles, and situations.

Adaptive communication, or "communication agility," is the art of adjusting how we express ourselves to fit our context and the people we're with. Research from psychologist Daniel Goleman, known for his work on emotional intelligence, highlights that adaptability is a key component of social intelligence. Goleman describes adaptive communication as essential for building trust and fostering mutual understanding across different settings. Adaptive communication is not about being inauthentic; it's about enhancing learning and ensuring our messages resonate more effectively. In this chapter, we will explore how to cultivate adaptability in communication, allowing us to connect meaningfully with people across various settings.

Why Adaptability in Communication Matters

I've often heard my mother say with confidence, "My daughter can adapt to any situation or group of people. Whether she's with children, the elderly, intellectuals, or learners, whether in a city or a village, she fits in, and everyone feels she belongs". For years, I heard these words without giving them much thought, but recently, I've begun to realize just how true they are.

Adaptability has been a guiding force in my life. Had I not embraced this quality, I wonder where I would be. Imagine a girl raised in one of the smallest villages in India, now a coach and a writer, sharing her experiences with people worldwide. My journey has shown me that adaptability isn't just a skill; it's an asset that opens doors to learning, connection, and growth in ways I'd never imagined.

The ability to adapt our communication style fosters trust, prevents misunderstandings, and creates an environment where people feel seen and heard. Adaptive communication bridges gaps between personality types, making collaborating with diverse teams easier, building stronger relationships, and encouraging open dialogue. A study published in the *Personality and Social Psychology Bulletin* found that people who adjusted their communication style based on their conversation partner's personality were rated likable, trustworthy, and competent.

Adaptability doesn't mean giving in, being submissive, or losing our individuality. It's not about abandoning our opinions or neglecting our own needs. Instead, adaptability is a powerful skill. It allows us to merge seamlessly into diverse environments while retaining our unique perspective. True adaptability stands out by choosing how to engage and connect with others. Far from compromising who we are, it empowers us to communicate in ways that bridge gaps, foster understanding, and build meaningful relationships.

Think about a recent conversation where you adjusted your communication style. How did this impact the flow and outcome of the interaction?

Deeper Dive: Handling Different Personality Types During Conflict

Conflicts can be challenging, especially when different personality types are involved. Knowing how to adapt communication styles during these times can significantly affect the outcome. Here are some strategies for handling common challenging personalities:

- *The Passive-Aggressive Type*: Address passive-aggressive behaviour by staying calm and asking open-ended questions to invite honest communication. For example, "I sense there's something more you'd like to share. Could you help me understand your perspective better?"

- *The Defensive Type:* When faced with someone who becomes defensive, acknowledge their feelings without placing blame. Use phrases like, "I understand this topic is important to you, and I want to find a solution together." This can help diffuse defensiveness and keep the conversation productive.

- *The Overly Dominant Type:* For dominant personalities, ensure everyone's voice is heard by politely but firmly setting boundaries. You might say, "I appreciate your input, but I'd also like to hear from others on this matter." This encourages balanced participation and prevents one person from overpowering the discussion.

Adapting to different personality types and using tailored strategies during conflicts can create an atmosphere conducive to resolution and understanding.

Understanding Different Communication Styles

It's essential to recognize various communication styles and understand how to approach them to communicate adaptively. While people are unique, these general styles provide a useful framework:

Analytical Communicators

Analytical communicators focus on facts, data, and logic. They appreciate structured conversations and evidence-based points, making them less receptive to emotional language or ambiguous ideas. When engaging with analytical communicators, being precise, concise, and clear is helpful.

- If you're presenting a proposal to an analytical communicator, provide clear data points and structured arguments, and avoid excessive emotional appeal. This clarity will build credibility and engagement.

Think of someone you know who is highly analytical. How can you incorporate clarity and evidence in your conversations with them?

Intuitive Communicators

Intuitive communicators enjoy exploring big-picture ideas, potential impacts, and possibilities. They may not focus on minute details but instead, value an overarching vision or goal. Framing ideas regarding broader impact or long-term goals can resonate well with them.

- When presenting a new project to an intuitive thinker, emphasize the vision and potential impact rather than focusing only on step-by-step processes.

Recall a conversation where focusing on the big picture resonated with someone. How did this approach enhance your connection?

Functional Communicators

Functional communicators appreciate details, processes, and step-by-step explanations. They feel most comfortable when conversations are structured and objectives are clear. Providing a plan or timeline helps create a smooth exchange.

- If you're working with a functional communicator, outlining the project in stages with clear objectives and deadlines can make them feel more secure and engaged.

Do you know someone who always seeks structure in conversations? How can you incorporate step-by-step clarity in discussions with them?

Personal Communicators

Personal communicators value emotional connection, rapport, and empathy. They connect through stories, shared experiences, and emotional resonance. Showing empathy, listening actively, and allowing space for open expression builds trust with personal communicators.

- When engaging with a personal communicator, share relevant stories or acknowledge emotions to create a stronger bond.

Consider a recent interaction where empathy and emotional engagement played a key role. How did this deepen your understanding of the other person?

Tailoring Your Communication for Context

I remember visiting a distant relative of my husband's in a village a few years back for the first time. As we were leaving, they mentioned they hadn't expected a professor like me to speak with such warmth and respect. I replied, "I didn't visit you as a professor today." If you can reach the heart of that statement, you'll understand the essence of adaptability. Too often, we carry a single image of ourselves wherever we go, and this rigidity can create unnecessary barriers. True adaptability means setting aside roles and labels when the situation calls for it, allowing genuine connection to flourish.

Context shapes how we communicate in a professional, social, or personal setting. Recognizing this shift allows us to adjust our tone, language, and focus to suit the environment and the expectations of those around us.

Professional Contexts: Communication in professional settings often needs to be clear, concise, and goal-oriented. Assertiveness, structure, and respect for formal boundaries are valued here. For instance, responding with focused attention and constructive input in a meeting keeps the conversation aligned with the objectives.

Social Contexts: Social settings are more informal, focusing on connection and shared experiences. Expressiveness, humour, and empathy are valued, fostering authenticity. Storytelling and active listening build rapport, reinforcing bonds in a relaxed environment.

Personal Contexts: Personal settings, like family interactions, require sensitivity and attentiveness. Empathy, patience, and responsiveness to emotional cues are key, as personal conversations often involve vulnerability and trust. Gentle approaches and affirmations such as "I understand" or "I'm here to listen" can deepen closeness.

Practical Strategies for Adaptive Communication

Adaptive communication skills involve practice, self-awareness, and a willingness to adjust our approach. Here are some practical strategies:

- *Practice Active Listening*: Fully engage with the speaker, maintaining eye contact and refraining from interrupting. Active listening shows respect and helps pick up cues about the other person's style.

  - Focus on understanding their perspective instead of planning your response.

- *Observe Non-Verbal Cues*: Body language, facial expressions, and tone provide insight into how others feel. Crossed arms may indicate discomfort, while nodding suggests agreement.

  - If someone seems disengaged, adjust your approach to re-engage them or invite their input.

- *Adjust Tone and Language*: Adapt your tone and language based on the context and person. A calm, assertive tone works well in formal settings, while a conversational tone suits casual gatherings.

  - Use inclusive language, like "we" or "our," in collaborative settings to foster teamwork.

- *Ask Open-Ended Questions*: Encourage others to share thoughts freely by asking questions that invite reflection.

  - Instead of "Do you agree?" try, "What are your thoughts on this?"

- *Stay Flexible and Non-Judgmental:* Let go of rigid expectations and open to different viewpoints, fostering more genuine responses.
  - If a conversation stalls, reassess your approach and be willing to pivot.

Adaptive Communication in Action

Imagine leading a team brainstorming session. Your team includes both detail-oriented members and big-picture thinkers. To adapt, you start by presenting a high-level vision for intuitive thinkers and a step-by-step outline for those who prefer structure. You encourage input from each team member, validating creative ideas and practical solutions. This adaptive approach creates a collaborative environment, enabling everyone to contribute naturally and feel valued.

Think of a time when you successfully adapted your communication style in a group setting. How did this approach impact the group's engagement and outcomes?

The Value of Flexibility in Communication

Adaptive communication is not just a skill; it's a mindset. It allows us to connect deeper, create inclusive environments, and build relationships grounded in respect. Each conversation enables us to practice and refine adaptability, making us more versatile and empathetic communicators. Remember, adaptive communication isn't about changing who we are; it's about enhancing how we connect, fostering authentic and lasting relationships across all areas of life.

Summary

This chapter emphasized the importance of adaptive communication, or the ability to shift communication styles based on context and the personalities involved. By understanding and adjusting to different communication styles - analytical, intuitive, functional, and personal. We can foster trust, prevent misunderstandings, and create meaningful connections. The chapter also highlighted strategies for navigating various contexts, including professional, social, and personal settings. It offered practical tips to develop adaptability, such as active listening, observing non-verbal cues, and asking open-ended questions. Adaptive communication was presented as a skill and mindset that empowers us to connect genuinely and effectively with diverse audiences.

Key Takeaways

- **Recognize and Adapt to Different Styles**: Understanding various communication styles enables us to adjust our approach, making connecting with others easier and fostering effective interactions.

- **Consider the Context**: Tailoring our communication to fit the context professional, social, or personal, enhances appropriateness and impact.

- **Use Active Listening and Observe Non-Verbal Cues**: Paying attention to non-verbal signals, such as body language and tone, while practicing active listening enriches our adaptability.

- **Ask Open-Ended Questions**: Open-ended questions invite others to share their thoughts, allowing us to respond thoughtfully and promote deeper conversations.

- **Stay Flexible and Open-Minded**: Letting go of rigid expectations and remaining open-minded allows us to respond authentically and build genuine connections.

Self-Reflection Questions

Reflect on your adaptive communication skills by considering the following questions:

1. How often do I adjust my communication style based on the person or context?

2. Do I actively listen and observe non-verbal cues to better understand others?

3. Am I open to changing my approach if a conversation isn't flowing well?

4. Do I encourage others to share their perspectives by asking open-ended questions?

5. How comfortable am I in shifting my tone, language, or approach based on the setting?

Self-Assessment Checklist

Rate each from 0 (Rarely) to 5 (Consistently):

1. I adjust my communication style to suit different situations and audiences effectively. ___ / 5

2. I am mindful of using clear and inclusive language that resonates with my audience. ___ / 5

3. I use storytelling as a tool to make my message relatable and memorable. ___ / 5

4. I adapt my tone and approach based on varying personalities and communication preferences. ___ / 5

5. I observe and respond to non-verbal cues to enhance understanding and connection. ___ / 5

Chapter 7

THE POWER OF NON-VERBAL COMMUNICATION

"What you do speaks so loudly that I cannot hear what you say."

—Ralph Waldo Emerson

Imagine walking into a room and instantly sensing the mood without a single word being spoken. Crossed arms, tense expressions, and averted eyes convey so much that words often fall short. This "silent language" of non-verbal communication frequently reveals the real story, expressing intentions, emotions, and attitudes that spoken words alone cannot capture.

In every interaction, non-verbal cues such as body language, tone of voice, spatial boundaries, and even moments of silence either enhance or contradict our spoken words. Studies in psychology and communication, like those conducted by Dr. Albert Mehrabian, reveal the profound impact of non-verbal cues on our perceptions. Mehrabian's research famously suggested that 93% of communication is non-verbal, emphasizing the importance of mastering this silent language for effective communication.

Observing non-verbal cues has become an inseparable part of my life, and this practice deepened significantly as I watched my students during speeches and presentations. I noticed that many of them were so focused on delivering content that they often overlooked vital elements of communication, such as body language, gestures, posture, eye contact, and even a simple smile.

As I honed this skill, I realized it allowed me to understand people more deeply. From their attire and accessories to the colour combinations they wear or the items they carry, such as bags, mobile phones, or watches, each detail can reveal insights into their personality, confidence, and even emotional state.

This journey of observing and adapting to non-verbal cues has profoundly influenced both my personal and professional life, enriching my interactions and fostering a more authentic connection with others. By becoming more attuned to these silent signals, I've seen that communication extends beyond words, creating profound, meaningful relationships and understanding.

Body Language: The Unspoken Message

Communication is more than just the words we use. Dr. Edward T. Hall, a pioneer in the field of non-verbal communication, introduced the concept of "proxemics", the study of personal space and distance in interactions. Hall's research highlights how our physical presence, from posture to spatial boundaries, conveys messages that words alone cannot express. Body language, whether it's the openness of a stance, the intensity of eye contact, or the subtle movements of our hands, speaks volumes about our intentions and emotions. Understanding and harnessing these non-verbal cues can transform our interactions, often communicating sincerity and confidence before we even speak.

Posture: Communicating Confidence or Discomfort

The way we hold ourselves speaks volumes about our mindset and emotional state. A straight, open posture conveys confidence, attentiveness, and readiness to engage while slouching or crossed arms can suggest defensiveness, discomfort, or even disinterest.

Cultural nuances also shape the interpretation of posture; in Western cultures, an upright stance often signals assertiveness, whereas in some Eastern contexts, it may be viewed as a sign of attentiveness and respect.

Why Posture Matters

Our posture influences how others perceive us because humans are wired to pick up on subtle cues to assess trustworthiness, confidence, and openness. An open posture makes us appear more approachable, signalling that we're ready to listen and engage. In contrast, a closed posture, like crossed arms, can unintentionally create a barrier, signalling that we may not be receptive to others' ideas or feedback. This subconscious interpretation often impacts first impressions and the tone of interactions.

Imagine yourself at a job interview, sitting straight and leaning slightly forward. This subtle shift in body language shows engagement and interest, creating a positive impression. Contrast this with leaning back with arms crossed, which might unintentionally convey detachment or unease, potentially affecting the interviewer's perception of your enthusiasm.

Quick Tips for Positive Body Language:

- Maintain an open posture to project confidence and attentiveness.
- Open gestures, such as uncrossed arms and hands visible, create warmth and approachability.
- Refrain from crossing your arms, as it can give off a closed or defensive impression.

Eye Contact: The Window to Connection

Eye contact is one of the most powerful forms of non-verbal communication, often called the "window to connection." We communicate attention, empathy, and sincerity through eye contact, making it essential for establishing trust. Studies indicate that people who maintain eye contact are often perceived as more genuine and engaged, fostering a sense of closeness and trustworthiness. However, interpretations of eye contact vary widely across cultures. In Western cultures, direct eye contact often signals confidence and honesty. In contrast, some Asian cultures view prolonged eye contact as potentially intrusive or even disrespectful, emphasizing that the meaning behind eye contact is culturally nuanced.

Example of Eye Contact in Practice

Imagine presenting a proposal to a client. You maintain steady eye contact as you speak, focusing on each participant as you address them. This creates a sense of involvement, encouraging engagement and signalling that you value their reactions. Imagine delivering the same presentation while constantly looking down or averting your gaze. The lack of eye contact can make you appear less confident or unprepared, potentially weakening the audience's trust and receptiveness.

Real-Life Scenario

Consider a job interview where the interviewer maintains strong eye contact, nodding and smiling at key moments. This level of engagement not only shows that they're actively listening but also helps to put you at ease. Contrast this with an interviewer who avoids eye contact, appearing distracted or disinterested. In this scenario, you may feel dismissed or undervalued, negatively impacting your responses and confidence.

Case Study

Eye contact's impact was notably observed in a customer service study where two groups of employees were trained in communication strategies, one with a focus on maintaining eye contact and the other without. Customers consistently rated the employees who maintained eye contact as friendlier, more helpful, and trustworthy. This shows that eye contact doesn't only influence professional perception but can also improve customer satisfaction and rapport in everyday interactions.

Navigating Cultural Differences

Eye contact in cross-cultural communication requires a careful balance to respect diverse norms. For instance, prolonged eye contact in Japan may be considered intrusive, signalling disrespect or confrontation. In some Middle Eastern cultures, sustained eye contact between men and women is often discouraged, as it may be viewed as overly intimate. Therefore, when interacting with people from different cultural backgrounds, it's wise to observe their comfort levels with eye contact and adjust accordingly.

Quick Tips for Eye Contact

- Maintain eye contact to convey confidence, sincerity, and attentiveness, but remember to blink naturally and avoid staring.

- Observe and adapt to cultural cues regarding eye contact. In some cultures, shorter, respectful glances may be more appropriate to respect personal boundaries.

- Aim for intervals of eye contact lasting about 3-5 seconds, breaking periodically to avoid making others uncomfortable.

Eye contact has the unique power to make others feel seen, valued, and connected. Mastering this skill enhances the authenticity of your communication and bridges cultural and personal boundaries, establishing a foundation for trust and genuine connection.

Tone of Voice: Communicating Emotion and Intent

How we say something often reveals our emotions and intentions just as much, if not more, than the words we use. Research suggests that tone contributes significantly to how a message is received, with pitch, volume, and pace expressing emotions from joy and calm to frustration and urgency. The tone of voice adds depth to our words, subtly communicating our emotional state and influencing how others interpret our intentions.

Modulating Pitch, Volume, and Pace

Understanding how to adjust pitch, volume, and pace can transform a simple message into an engaging and impactful one. For example, a steady, calm tone builds trust and conveys control, while a loud or rushed tone can imply urgency or even anxiety. Modulating these aspects is especially effective in public speaking, where maintaining clarity and emotional engagement is crucial.

Imagine a scenario where a manager provides feedback to an employee. If the manager speaks in a low, steady pitch, with a calm and measured pace, the feedback is likely to be perceived as constructive and supportive. However, if the same message is delivered in a louder, faster tone, it may come across as critical or impatient, leaving the employee feeling defensive rather than receptive. In this case, tone of voice directly influences how the feedback is received. A study on healthcare communication demonstrated how tone of voice affects patient trust and satisfaction. Doctors who spoke in a calm, empathetic tone saw significantly higher levels of patient trust and engagement than those who spoke quickly or sharply, even if the information provided was identical. This study highlights that tone can create a comforting environment where people feel heard and valued, particularly in sensitive conversations.

Tone in Different Contexts:

Our tone of voice often needs to change depending on the situation. A clear and confident tone generally fosters respect and attentiveness in professional settings. However, in personal or supportive conversations, a warmer, softer tone may more effectively convey empathy and understanding. Recognizing the right tone for each context allows us to communicate more effectively, meeting the emotional needs of our audience.

Quick Tips for a Thoughtful Tone of Voice

- **Lower Your Pitch for Calmness and Authority**: A slightly lower pitch can project calmness and authority, making your message sound more assured and creating a calming effect. This approach is particularly helpful in high-stress situations or leadership roles.

- **Slow Down for Emphasis**: When discussing crucial points, slow down your speech to emphasize their importance. This gives others time to absorb and reflect on what you're saying, enhancing clarity and impact.

- **Adopt a Warm Tone in Supportive Conversations**: In sensitive discussions, using a warm, gentle tone can help reassure others, making them feel comfortable and open to sharing. This approach is especially effective in personal relationships or coaching scenarios.

- **Reflect on Tone and Intent**: Consider a recent conversation was there a noticeable difference between what was said and how it was said? For example, a phrase like "I'm fine" can sound sincere, dismissive, or frustrated, depending on tone alone. Reflecting on these moments can help you become more mindful of how your tone impacts others.

The tone of voice plays an influential role in communication, influencing how others perceive our words and how they feel during interactions. By mastering our tone, we can convey empathy, clarity, and confidence, making our messages impactful and memorable.

Proxemics: Respecting Boundaries

Proxemics, or the use of space in communication, dramatically influences how comfortable and connected we feel during interactions. Cultural norms, personal preferences, and situational context deeply shape our sense of personal space. For instance, people from Mediterranean and Latin American cultures may feel comfortable standing closer during conversations, emphasizing warmth and connection. In contrast, individuals from Northern European cultures often prefer maintaining more personal space, valuing a sense of privacy and respect. Understanding these differences allows us to adapt our interactions to make others feel at ease and respected.

Zones of Proximity

1. **Intimate Distance**

   This zone is reserved for close friends, family members, and romantic partners, where personal connection is most substantial. At this distance, physical touch and quiet conversations are common.

- *Example*: Think of comforting a close friend in distress. Moving into intimate distance allows you to offer a supportive hug or comforting touch on the shoulder, reinforcing emotional closeness.

2. **Personal Distance**

Commonly used in everyday, friendly conversations, personal distance provides enough space to engage without invading someone's privacy. This distance feels comfortable for casual discussions with friends or colleagues.

- *Example*: During a catch-up with a friend over coffee, maintaining a personal distance allows you to have an engaging conversation while respecting each other's personal space.

3. **Social Distance**

This zone is ideal for professional or formal interactions. Personal boundaries are respected at this distance, creating a balanced dynamic that maintains formality while allowing easy communication.

- *Example*: Maintaining a social distance from colleagues in a business meeting conveys professionalism. You may sit across a table or maintain a few feet's distance when discussing a project, signalling respect and a focus on business.

4. **Public Distance**

Typically used in public speaking or more extensive group settings, public distance allows for a formal, structured communication dynamic where the speaker can address multiple people simultaneously.

- *Example*: During a presentation to a larger audience, keeping a public distance allows the speaker to address the crowd effectively, ensuring that their voice carries and that each audience member can see them comfortably without feeling crowded.

Quick Tips for Proxemics

- **In Professional Settings**: Try to maintain a respectful social distance that conveys professionalism without feeling distant. For example, in meetings, staying at a social distance can foster approachability while maintaining formality.

- **Cultural Sensitivity**: When interacting across cultures, adjust your proximity based on cultural norms to ensure comfort. If you're speaking with someone from a culture that values more personal space, stepping back slightly can help them feel at ease.

- **In Personal Contexts**: Use closeness thoughtfully to build intimacy without overstepping. Moving slightly closer during empathetic moments or personal sharing can help strengthen a bond, but be mindful of the other person's body language to avoid discomfort. Think about a time when someone stood either too close or too far from you. Did their proximity make you feel uneasy, or did it foster a sense of connection? Reflecting on these experiences can help you become more attuned to the impact of space in communication, enhancing your ability to navigate social boundaries with sensitivity and respect.

Artefacts and Appearance: Conveying Identity and Intentions

The items we wear or display, such as clothing, accessories, and even workspace décor, serve as nonverbal cues that reveal aspects of our identity, values, and intentions. For instance, a lawyer in formal attire communicates professionalism and attention to detail, while casual wear suggests a more relaxed, approachable persona. These intentional or subconscious artefacts shape others' perceptions of us, subtly influencing their expectations about who we are and how we might interact.

Real-Life Scenario

Consider a CEO attending a critical industry event. If they arrive in a formal suit, they project authority and command respect, encouraging others to treat them with a certain level of deference. However, wearing jeans and a t-shirt may make them more approachable and down-to-earth, possibly inviting more casual and open interactions. This choice of attire not only influences how others perceive them but also sets the tone for engagement, demonstrating how appearance can impact communication dynamics.

Examples of Artefacts in Professional and Personal Contexts

1. *Professional Attire:* In corporate environments, formal clothing like suits or business attire communicates professionalism, seriousness, and reliability. For example, a job candidate in a neatly tailored suit conveys a strong intent to impress and succeed. In contrast, a candidate dressed in overly casual attire may give the impression that they're less committed to the role.

2. *Personal Accessories:* Small choices, such as the type of watch, jewellery, or even a bag, can shape how others interpret our personality. An elegant, understated watch might convey sophistication and discipline, while brightly coloured, bold accessories could signal creativity and expressiveness.

3. *Workspace Decor:* The items we choose to display in our workspace such as motivational quotes, plants, or even family photos offer insights into our priorities and values. For instance, a desk filled with family pictures suggests a person who values close relationships, while minimalistic decor may emphasise order and simplicity.

Quick Tips for Using Appearance Thoughtfully

- *Dress According to Context:* Tailor your attire to fit the situation. Formal attire helps establish authority and respect in professional settings, while casual wear suits more relaxed environments. When uncertain, it's often better to lean slightly toward formality to avoid appearing underprepared.

- *Respect Cultural Norms:* Clothing can carry significant cultural meaning, so it's essential to consider these nuances, especially in multicultural settings. Some cultures view specific attire as disrespectful or inappropriate, and demonstrating awareness of these norms shows respect and cultural sensitivity.

- *Select Accessories Mindfully:* Opt for simple, elegant accessories to enhance rather than distract from your message in professional environments. Flashy or overly elaborate items may draw attention away from your words, while subtle choices reinforce professionalism.

Think back to when someone's appearance influenced your first impression of them. What message did their clothing or accessories convey? Did they seem approachable, professional, or perhaps indifferent? Reflecting on these experiences can make us more mindful of the messages we send through our appearance, helping us align our presentation with our intentions.

The Power of Silence

Though often overlooked, silence is one of the most potent tools in non-verbal communication. A well-timed pause in a conversation can signal reflection, empathy, or even tension, depending on the context. Silence is not merely the absence of words; it can carry significant weight, often conveying emotions or intentions that words cannot capture. Studies have shown that silence can have a profound impact on interactions. For example, research published in the *Journal of Social and Personal Relationships* indicates that intentional pauses or moments of silence can increase perceived attentiveness and empathy, leading to deeper, more meaningful connections between people.

Silence also has cultural nuances. In Japan, for instance, silence is highly valued as a sign of respect and thoughtfulness, allowing people to consider their responses carefully. In many Western cultures, however, prolonged silence can create discomfort, as people are often accustomed to filling gaps in conversation. Recognizing these cultural differences can help us use silence effectively and respect others' boundaries.

Real-Life Reflection

Think of a time when you used silence intentionally to convey a message. Perhaps you paused after delivering an important point to let it sink in or held back your words to allow someone else to process their emotions. Did it help to emphasize your point, show empathy, or create a moment for reflection? When used thoughtfully, silence can bring depth to a conversation, fostering a sense of presence and connection. One of my earliest lessons in the power of silence came from my childhood. Whenever I made a mistake, my mother stopped talking instead of scolding or explaining. At first, her silence puzzled me; I wondered what had gone wrong. Over time, I would realize that I had done something she disapproved of, and the silence would prompt me to reflect on my actions. When I finally approached her, she opened the conversation, allowing me to understand my mistake without reprimanding.

This experience taught me the profound impact of silence as a communication tool. Over the years, I've adopted a similar approach, using silence when words might be unnecessary or counterproductive. Silence has a unique way of inviting self-reflection, allowing both parties to process emotions and thoughts. I'm certain many of you have experienced something similar, perhaps when someone avoided speaking to you or ignored your messages to convey their feelings. These moments remind us that silence often communicates more powerfully than words.

Quick Tips for Using Silence Effectively

- *Pause to Emphasize Key Points:* After making an important statement, a brief pause can help your message resonate. Silence gives others time to process and reflect on what you've said, enhancing the impact of your words.

- *Allow Silence After Asking Questions:* When you ask a question, resist the urge to fill the silence immediately. Allowing a quiet moment gives the other person space to think, often leading to more thoughtful and authentic responses.

- *Respect Silence in Sensitive Conversations:* Silence can show empathy and understanding in emotional or sensitive discussions. Giving others time to process their emotions before responding communicates that you're present and supportive without pressing for immediate answers.

Consider how silence has shaped your life. Have there been moments when someone's silence spoke louder than their words? Or times when your silence conveyed understanding, patience, or disappointment? Reflecting on these experiences can help you appreciate the subtle power of silence and integrate it more consciously into your communication.

Harnessing the Power of Non-verbal Communication

Non-verbal communication is the foundation that often speaks louder than words. The unspoken language reveals our intentions, emotions, and sincerity, shaping how our messages are perceived long before we articulate them. By becoming more aware of our body language, tone, spatial boundaries, silence, and even subtle environmental cues, we can communicate with greater empathy, clarity, and effectiveness. This awareness allows us to foster connections that are not only meaningful but also deeply resonant, helping us connect on a more authentic level.

The next time you engage in a conversation, take a moment to look beyond words. Notice the unspoken elements your gestures, posture, eye contact, and tone. Are they reinforcing your message or creating ambiguity? Mastering this silent language opens the door to a world of empathy, engagement, and understanding, enabling you to convey authenticity and respect.

In a world where words can sometimes fall short, non-verbal communication is the bridge that ensures our intentions are heard, seen, and truly felt. By harnessing the power of this "silent" language, we become more attuned communicators, capable of easily building trust and rapport. This practice of mindful, non-verbal awareness elevates not just our conversations but the quality of our relationships, allowing us to connect in ways that words alone cannot achieve.

Understanding Non-Verbal Cues: Common Gestures, Postures, and Their Meanings

These interpretations represent common, generalized meanings of non-verbal cues, but individual expressions can vary widely based on personal habits, context, and cultural backgrounds. It's always best to consider these cues as part of a broader communication context.

Positive/Engaging Non-Verbal Cues

Non-Verbal Cue	Meaning or Interpretation	Notes
Open Palm Gestures	Honesty, openness, or trustworthiness	Often used in greetings to convey transparency and sincerity.
Nodding	Agreement, active listening	Can show engagement and understanding, though excessive nodding may appear insincere.
Leaning Forward	Engagement, interest	Indicates attentiveness; be cautious of leaning too close as it may feel intrusive.
Firm Handshake	Confidence, assertiveness	Shows a positive first impression; weak handshakes may signal insecurity.
Eye Contact	Confidence, attentiveness, respect	Balancing eye contact shows respect, though overdoing it may seem intense.

Smiling	Friendliness, warmth, openness	Genuine smiles involve eye muscles ("Duchenne" smile), while forced smiles appear insincere.
Mirroring Body Language	Rapport, connection, empathy	Subconsciously reflects others' gestures to build rapport.
Head Tilt	Interest, empathy	Shows curiosity and attentiveness when actively listening.
Standing with Feet Apart	Confidence, stability, assertiveness	A wide stance signals groundedness and balance.
Hand to Heart Gesture	Sincerity, honesty, apology	Used to show genuine emotion, often during apologies or public speaking.
Hands Clasped Together	Thoughtfulness, anticipation	May show readiness or interest when combined with forward posture.
Maintaining Personal Space	Respectfulness, awareness of cultural norms	Observing others' comfort zones fosters ease and professionalism.
Open Body Posture	Receptiveness, openness	Avoids closed or defensive positioning, creating a welcoming impression.
Nodding with Soft Smile	Encouragement, engagement	Positive reinforcement that invites further sharing in a conversation.

Negative/Defensive Non-Verbal Cues

Non-Verbal Cue	Meaning or Interpretation	Notes
Crossed Arms	Defensive, closed-off, discomfort	It is common in uncomfortable situations but sometimes a habit for physical comfort.
Leaning Back	Disinterest, boredom, or disengagement	It can also show confidence depending on context but is often seen as distancing.
Avoiding Eye Contact	Nervousness, discomfort, lack of interest	It is common in situations of discomfort, but in some cultures, it shows respect.
Finger Pointing	Aggression, assertiveness, accusation	Often seen as aggressive and disrespectful.
Touching or Rubbing Nose	Discomfort, nervousness, possible dishonesty	Often linked to lying, though it may simply indicate nervousness or itching.
Biting Nails	Nervousness, anxiety, or stress	A self-soothing gesture often seen when someone is anxious or focused.
Playing with Object or Hair	Nervousness, boredom, or flirtation	Can be a self-soothing action or show casual engagement; context is key.
Crossed Legs (Away)	Defensive, disinterest	Facing away from someone may signal distancing or discomfort.

Shrugging Shoulders	Indifference, uncertainty	Signals a lack of concern or knowledge, often perceived as non-committal.
Touching Face or Hair	Nervousness, self-soothing, insecurity	Often done subconsciously in uncomfortable or tense situations.
Fidgeting	Nervousness, impatience, or boredom	Common in stressful situations; may be perceived as a lack of focus or unease.
Tapping Fingers or Foot	Impatience, boredom	Often signals restlessness or annoyance.
Looking Down or Away	Insecurity, shyness, submissiveness	May indicate a lack of confidence or feeling overwhelmed in certain contexts.
Covering Mouth	Surprise, shock, hesitation	Often done instinctively, especially in surprise or hesitation.
Slouching or Poor Posture	Disinterest, low energy	Generally perceived as lacking confidence or attentiveness.

Summary

Non-verbal communication is a powerful, often unspoken language that can amplify, clarify, or even contradict our words. This chapter examined the essential elements of non-verbal cues, including body language, tone of voice, personal space, appearance, and the strategic use of silence. By understanding and consciously applying these aspects of non-verbal communication, we can connect more effectively, foster stronger relationships, and convey our messages with authenticity and impact.

Key Takeaways

- **Non-verbal Cues Complement Verbal Messages**: Elements like body language, eye contact, and tone significantly influence how our words are received, often shaping the entire meaning of a conversation.

- **Body Language and Tone Are Crucial**: Posture, facial expressions, gestures, and tone play a significant role in shaping perceptions, and their meanings can vary widely across different cultural contexts.

- **Respecting Personal Space (Proxemics)**: Adjusting our physical proximity based on personal and cultural norms helps maintain comfort and professionalism, especially in diverse settings.

- **Silence as a Powerful Communication Tool**: Thoughtful pauses allow for reflection, convey empathy, and emphasize important points, adding depth to sensitive conversations.

- **Artefacts and Appearance Matter**: Choices in attire, personal accessories, and even environmental cues subtly communicate intentions and can enhance or detract from our intended message.

Self-Reflection Checklist

Rate each from 0 (Rarely) to 5 (Consistently):

1. I am mindful of my body language and ensure it aligns with my spoken words. ___ / 5

2. I make an effort to maintain appropriate eye contact during conversations. ___ / 5

3. I use my tone of voice effectively to convey the intended emotion and emphasis. ___ / 5

4. I am aware of personal space and adjust it respectfully according to cultural and situational norms. ___ / 5

5. I consciously choose attire and surroundings that support my intended message. ___ / 5

Chapter 8

NEGOTIATION - THE COMMUNICATION SKILL THAT CHANGES EVERYTHING

"In life, you don't get what you deserve. You get what you negotiate."

—Chester L. Karrass.

Negotiation is more than a tactic for boardrooms and business deals; it is a life skill woven into everyday interactions. From navigating workplace discussions to resolving household conflicts, negotiation shapes how we balance needs, build relationships, and achieve goals. It's not just about getting what you want; it's about finding common ground, fostering collaboration, and crafting outcomes that work for all parties involved.

A manager overseeing a project faces an unexpected delay. Rather than issuing orders or succumbing to frustration, they approach the client with a composed strategy. "We've encountered some unforeseen challenges," they explain, "but we've identified solutions that can keep us on track with a slightly adjusted timeline. Would you be open to discussing these options?" This simple yet intentional approach transforms a potentially tense situation into a collaborative conversation, preserving trust and paving the way for success.

Effective negotiation requires a blend of empathy, clarity, and adaptability. It's about truly understanding the other party's needs while articulating your own with confidence and respect. Research published in *Harvard Business Review* emphasizes that negotiation is not just a tool for resolving conflicts but a pathway to building stronger, more dynamic relationships.

In this chapter, we'll explore how negotiation is not a zero-sum game but a bridge to mutual understanding. Through real-life examples, practical strategies, and insightful techniques, you'll discover how mastering negotiation can empower you to navigate challenging conversations, achieve meaningful outcomes, and foster lasting connections.

What is Negotiation?

Negotiation is the art of reaching mutual agreement while balancing differing interests, goals, and perspectives. At its core, negotiation is not about winning or losing; it is about crafting outcomes that align with shared values and objectives. Whether it's a professional salary discussion or resolving a disagreement with a friend, negotiation is a dynamic process that requires skill, empathy, and adaptability.

Key Elements of Negotiation

Mastering negotiation involves understanding its essential elements, each playing a vital role in steering discussions toward meaningful outcomes:

1. **Preparation: Setting the Stage:** Preparation is the cornerstone of any successful negotiation. You can enter the discussion with clarity and confidence by understanding your goals, the other party's interests, and the potential outcomes.

    - Before negotiating a job offer, research industry standards, identify your value to the company, and outline your priorities, such as salary, benefits, or growth opportunities.

2. **Active Listening: Hearing Beyond Words:** Effective negotiation involves understanding the other party's underlying concerns and motivations. Active listening creates a space for collaboration and builds trust.

   - In a dispute between colleagues, listening to each person's concerns about workload helps uncover the root of the conflict, enabling a fair and effective resolution.

3. **Emotional Intelligence: Managing the Moment:** Emotional intelligence allows negotiators to navigate tense moments with composure. Recognizing and regulating emotions ensures that discussions remain constructive rather than confrontational.

   - During a heated budget meeting, a leader notices rising tension and pauses to validate the team's frustrations before calmly refocusing on solutions.

4. **Clarity and Persuasion: The Power of Communication:** Clear and persuasive communication ensures your points are understood without creating resistance. It's about articulating your needs while respecting the other party's perspective.

   - When requesting a deadline extension, explaining the challenges clearly and offering a detailed revised timeline demonstrates accountability and fosters understanding.

The Psychology of Negotiation

Negotiation is as much about understanding human behaviour as it is about articulating terms. The underlying psychology of how people think, feel, and react can shape the course of a negotiation, making it crucial to understand the human element involved.

At its core, negotiation taps into fundamental psychological principles that drive human interaction. Recognizing and leveraging these behaviours can create an environment conducive to reaching mutual agreements.

1. **The Need to Be Heard and Valued**

   People enter negotiations with goals, emotions, and expectations. When individuals feel heard, respected, and valued, they are more likely to engage constructively. Acknowledge the other party's perspective by summarizing their concerns before presenting your point of view. This validation fosters openness.

   - In a workplace salary discussion, starting with, "I understand how tight budgets have been recently," shows empathy, making your request more palatable.

2. **Anchoring Bias: Setting the Tone Early**

   Anchoring bias refers to the psychological effect of the first offer made in a negotiation. This initial anchor often frames the range within which the discussion occurs. Use anchors strategically. Set an opening offer that favours your position while leaving room for negotiation, but ensure it remains reasonable to avoid disengagement.

   - A real estate agent sets the initial listing price slightly above market value, knowing potential buyers will anchor their offers around it.

3. **Reciprocity: The Power of Concessions**

   The principle of reciprocity suggests that small concessions can inspire similar gestures from the other party, fostering a collaborative dynamic. Start by offering something of value, whether flexibility, additional terms, or even goodwill. This often encourages the other party to respond in kind.

- A vendor negotiating contract terms offers to waive setup fees, prompting the client to agree to an extended service agreement.

Building Trust and Rapport

Trust is the cornerstone of successful negotiations. Without it, even well-intentioned offers can be met with scepticism. Establishing rapport transforms adversarial discussions into collaborative problem-solving.

1. **Techniques for Creating a Collaborative Environment**

   - *Transparency:* Be open about your goals and constraints to foster trust.

   - *Common Ground:* Highlight shared interests or goals to create a sense of alignment.

   - *Non-Verbal Communication:* Maintain steady eye contact, use open body language, and nod in agreement to signal understanding and collaboration.

Imagine a sales representative negotiating with a prospective client. The representative builds credibility by openly discussing a product's pros and cons. They further enhance trust by suggesting a pilot program to test the solution before full implementation. This honest and collaborative approach seals the deal and establishes a long-term partnership.

By understanding human behaviour, recognizing psychological tendencies like anchoring and reciprocity, and building trust, negotiators can create an environment of mutual respect and collaboration. This approach transforms negotiation from a tactical exercise into a meaningful interaction where both parties leave satisfied.

Types of Negotiation

Understanding the different types of negotiation is essential for tailoring your approach to specific scenarios. Each type is characterized by the parties' dynamics, goals, and desired outcomes.

1. **Distributive Negotiation (Win-Lose):** Distributive negotiation, often called "zero-sum," revolves around dividing a fixed amount of resources. In this scenario, one party's gain is the other party's loss.

   - **Key Characteristics**
     - Focuses on claiming value rather than creating it.
     - Typically involves a single issue, like price or quantity.
     - Common in short-term or one-off transactions.
   - Negotiating the price of a car. A buyer and a seller negotiate over the cost of a vehicle. The buyer aims to lower the price as much as possible, while the seller wants to maximize profit. There's no emphasis on creating additional value or fostering a future relationship.
   - **Strategy:** Use anchoring effectively to understand the other party's bottom line to gain leverage.

2. **Integrative Negotiation (Win-Win):** Integrative negotiation seeks to create value by addressing the needs and interests of both parties and achieving mutually beneficial outcomes.

   - **Key Characteristics**
     - Focuses on collaboration and finding creative solutions.
     - Involves multiple issues that can be negotiated to maximize overall value.
     - Encourages open communication and transparency.

- Two departments collaborating to share resources for a joint project. Department A has extra workspace, while Department B has specialized equipment. By pooling these resources, both departments can benefit from achieving their goals without additional costs.

- **Strategy:** Identify shared goals and explore areas where trade-offs can enhance both parties' outcomes.

3. **Collaborative Negotiation:** Collaborative negotiation is a refined approach beyond merely seeking mutual benefits. It focuses on building trust and establishing enduring relationships. It is particularly relevant in contexts where the negotiation parties have an ongoing connection, such as partnerships, long-term business alliances, or close personal relationships.

   In collaborative negotiation, the emphasis is on solving immediate problems and creating a foundation for future cooperation. Unlike distributive negotiation, where resources are divided, or integrative negotiation, which seeks win-win outcomes, collaborative negotiation aligns interests in ways that benefit both parties over time.

   - Two departments within a company need to share a limited budget. Instead of competing for funds, they discuss their individual priorities. Department A agrees to reduce its allocation for marketing materials, while Department B reallocates some of its resources to support A's upcoming event. Together, they create a solution that benefits both teams.

   - **Strategy:** Focus on shared goals by identifying mutual interests. Start the conversation by saying, "How can we ensure both our needs are met while maximizing the overall benefit?" This sets a collaborative tone and encourages creative problem-solving.

Aspects of Collaborative Negotiation:

1. **Shared Vision**: Collaborative negotiators work to establish a shared understanding of long-term goals. For example, two companies forming a strategic partnership may focus on immediate deliverables and building market influence over the next five years.

2. **Trust Building**: Transparency, honesty, and reliability are critical. Sharing relevant information without fear of exploitation fosters trust, making future collaborations smoother.

3. **Creative Problem-Solving**: By prioritizing mutual interests, parties explore innovative solutions beyond the obvious, leading to outcomes that benefit both.

4. **Emotional Intelligence**: Recognizing and managing emotions are critical to respect and understanding, even during disagreements.

Strategies for Effective Negotiation

Prepare Thoroughly: Before entering the discussion, understand your goals, the other party's needs, and potential outcomes.

Prioritize Active Listening: Pay attention to verbal and non-verbal cues to uncover underlying interests and concerns.

Manage Emotions: Stay calm and composed, using emotional intelligence to diffuse tension and maintain focus on solutions.

Frame Proposals Effectively: Present your points clearly, emphasizing mutual benefits and aligning with the other party's interests.

Be Open to Creative Solutions: Flexibility and willingness to explore alternatives can lead to win-win outcomes and strengthen relationships.

Practical Tools and Techniques for Negotiation

Effective negotiation requires not just theoretical understanding but also the application of practical tools and techniques. These methods can enhance your ability to communicate, build rapport, and achieve mutually beneficial outcomes. Here are some essential tools to sharpen your negotiation skills:

1. **BATNA (Best Alternative to a Negotiated Agreement):** BATNA is your backup plan, which means the best outcome you can turn to if the negotiation doesn't go your way. Knowing this gives you clarity and confidence because you have a clear idea of what you'll do if an agreement isn't reached.

   - *Application:* if you're negotiating a salary and your BATNA is accepting another job offer with a specific pay, you're less likely to take an unsatisfactory deal in the current negotiation. It ensures you don't settle for less than what's reasonable for you.

2. **The Power of Silence:** Pauses can be surprisingly powerful. Strategic silence allows you to gather your thoughts, make the other party reconsider their stance, or encourage them to reveal more information.

   - *Application:* During a salary negotiation, pausing after presenting your expected figure can create space for the employer to respond, often leading to more favourable outcomes.

3. **The 70-30 Rule:** Effective negotiators listen 70% of the time and speak 30%. Listening actively provides insights into the other party's needs, concerns, and motivations, which you can use to guide the discussion.

   - *Application:* In a business deal, use the 70-30 rule to uncover the client's underlying priorities, enabling you to tailor your proposal effectively.

4. **Role-Playing Scenarios:** Practicing negotiation scenarios with a mentor, colleague, or trusted peer helps refine your skills and prepare you for challenging discussions.

    - *Application:* If you're preparing to negotiate a contract, role-play with a friend who acts as the counterparty. Simulate objections and practice responses to build confidence.

These practical tools and techniques provide a framework for approaching negotiations with confidence, adaptability, and precision. You can successfully navigate even the most challenging conversations by applying them consistently.

Measuring Success in Negotiation

Evaluating the success of a negotiation goes beyond simply achieving your desired outcome or "winning." True success in negotiation lies in balancing the results with the quality of the relationship and the lessons learned for future interactions. Here are key aspects to reflect on after a negotiation:

- **Was the Relationship Strengthened?**

  Consider whether the negotiation fostered trust, mutual respect, and collaboration. Strengthened relationships lead to long-term partnerships and future opportunities.

  - *Reflection:* Did the tone of the conversation build rapport, or did it create tension? How did your approach influence this dynamic?

- **Were Goals Met, or Was Progress Made?**

  Assess whether the negotiation achieved its objectives or made significant progress toward them. Even partial agreements can be valuable if they pave the way for future collaboration.

- *Reflection:* Were your goals clearly articulated and understood by all parties? Did the outcome align with your expectations or surpass them?

- **What Could Be Improved in Future Negotiations?**

  Reflect on your performance to identify areas of improvement, whether in preparation, communication, or emotional control. Consider how you could apply these lessons in upcoming discussions.

  - *Reflection:* Were there moments where better preparation or different strategies could have yielded better results? What feedback would you give yourself?

Reflecting on these aspects ensures continuous growth in your negotiation skills. It transforms each experience, regardless of the outcome, into a valuable learning opportunity, enabling you to build stronger relationships and achieve tremendous success in future negotiations.

Given all the tips, tricks, and techniques discussed, one essential truth stands out: authenticity is key. Genuine efforts to create a mutually beneficial outcome are rarely in vain. One incident during my time as a university professor still stands out vividly, illustrating this principle.

During the COVID-19 pandemic, when online lectures were the norm, a challenging situation arose. A batch of students was required to complete a portion of the syllabus and submit assignments within two days. Unsurprisingly, the students were overwhelmed; they had other deadlines, commitments, and exam preparation to tackle. Their frustration turned into outright rebellion. They appealed to the Head of the Department to cancel the classes and assignments entirely, refusing to cooperate.

Recognizing the complexity of the situation, the Head asked me to step in. In an online meeting with the students and the Head present, I approached the matter with empathy and authenticity. I began by genuinely listening to their concerns, acknowledging their frustrations, and appreciating their courage to voice their challenges openly. This initial step set a positive tone, easing the tension.

Next, I highlighted the university and professors' efforts to support students during those critical times. This was not to justify their demands but to foster a shared understanding of the situation. Then, I asked specific questions: "Which aspects of the course and assignments are most challenging for you? Why do you feel the current plan is unmanageable?" This allowed me to uncover the root of their concerns.

Having understood their struggles, I proposed a compromise. I suggested minor modifications to the assignment structure, making it more manageable and time-efficient without compromising academic objectives. The students were receptive and appreciative of the effort to meet them halfway. By the end of the meeting, we had an agreement with which everyone was satisfied.

Afterward, the Department head personally commended my approach, noting how it had turned a potential conflict into a collaborative solution. One important lesson is that negotiation is not about "winning" a conversation. It is a skill, a tool, and an asset we must develop in such a way that, even if we lose a battle, we ultimately win the war.

Summary

Negotiation-The Communication Skill That Changes Everything

Negotiation has proven an essential communication skill, extending beyond boardroom deals into everyday interactions such as resolving personal conflicts or achieving professional goals. Far from being a zero-sum game, negotiation has been described as a collaborative process that balances empathy, clarity, and adaptability to craft outcomes beneficial to all parties. It is about winning, fostering trust, building relationships, and achieving meaningful progress.

This chapter explored the psychology of negotiation, emphasizing the importance of understanding human behaviour, such as the need to feel heard and the principles of reciprocity. It also examined different types of negotiation, distributive, integrative, and collaborative, while offering strategies and tools like BATNA, active listening, and the power of silence. Reflecting on negotiation outcomes encouraged continuous learning and growth, transforming challenges into opportunities for deeper connections and success.

Key Takeaways

1. **Negotiation as a Collaborative Skill**: Successful negotiation prioritizes mutual understanding and shared goals over competition.

2. **Psychological Insights Matter**: Understanding human behaviour, such as anchoring bias and reciprocity, enhances the likelihood of favourable outcomes.

3. **Types of Negotiation**: Recognizing the differences between distributive, integrative, and collaborative negotiation helps tailor approaches to specific contexts.

4. **Effective Strategies**: Preparation, active listening, and emotional intelligence are critical for challenging discussions.

5. **Reflection Ensures Growth**: Evaluating negotiation outcomes fosters continuous improvement in skills and relationships.

Reflection Activity

Take time to reflect on your recent negotiations and consider the following questions:

1. What approach did I use (distributive, integrative, or collaborative), and was it effective?

2. Did I prioritize understanding the other party's perspective and how it influenced the outcome?

3. Can I manage my emotions and maintain composure during tense moments?

4. What tools or strategies did I apply, and were they successful?

5. How can I improve my preparation or communication in future negotiations?

Self-Assessment Checklist

Rate Yourself from 0 (Rarely) to 5 (Consistently):

1. I prepare thoroughly by understanding my goals, the other party's needs, and possible outcomes. ___ / 5

2. I actively listen and respond to the underlying concerns of the other party. ___ / 5

3. I manage my emotions and remain composed during tense discussions. ___ / 5

4. I communicate my points persuasively and without aggression. ___ / 5

5. I reflect on the success and lessons of my negotiations to improve future outcomes. ___ / 5

Part 2: Transforming How You Communicate with Others, Situational Skill Building

Instructions: Reflect on each scenario and use skills from Part 2, focusing on clarity, handling tough conversations, and effectively managing Nonverbal cues.

- *A family member makes a comment that feels critical, but you're unsure if it was intentional. How could you initiate a respectful conversation to address it without escalating tensions?*

- *You're giving feedback to a co-worker whose performance needs improvement. How would you approach this with clarity and empathy, ensuring the feedback is constructive?*

- *When a friend shares something personal with you, your first reaction is to give advice. How would you pause and practice empathetic listening instead, allowing them to feel truly heard?*

- *In a team meeting, you notice a colleague is disengaged, crossing their arms and looking away. Describe how you would approach this, using Non-verbal cues to foster a more collaborative environment.*

- *During a family discussion, a relative interrupts you multiple times. How could you assertively but gently ask for space to complete your thoughts, showing respect while maintaining clear boundaries?*

- *You need to approach your manager about a decision you don't agree with. Consider how you would communicate your perspective assertively while respecting their authority and keeping the conversation open to different viewpoints.*

PART 3

COMMUNICATION IN THE MODERN WORLD

> *"The art of communication is the language of leadership."*
>
> — James Humes.

In a fast-paced, digitally-driven world, communication has evolved significantly. Modern personal or professional interactions require heightened awareness, adaptability, and cultural sensitivity. Technology has expanded our reach and created countless opportunities for connection, but it has also introduced challenges, misinterpretations, distractions, and barriers to genuine engagement.

This part explores the complexities of communication in the modern era, equipping you with the tools to navigate its dynamic landscape. Whether fostering online relationships, bridging cultural divides, or demonstrating emotional intelligence in a virtual meeting, Part 3 empowers you to lead and connect effectively in an interconnected world.

In this section, you'll discover how to:

- **Leverage Digital Communication**: Master the art of clear, thoughtful online interactions that build trust and foster meaningful connections across screens.

- **Adapt to Cultural Diversity**: Understand and respect cultural nuances, fostering inclusivity and collaboration in diverse settings.

- **Cultivate Emotional Intelligence**: Develop self-awareness and empathy to navigate complex interactions with authenticity, bridging gaps in understanding and creating lasting bonds.

Think of Part 3 as your roadmap to managing the nuances of modern communication. By embracing these principles, you'll be equipped to build relationships that transcend borders, inspire collaboration, and foster compassion in every conversation.

In a world where rapid exchanges often replace deep dialogue, this part encourages you to pause, reflect, and bring intentionality to your communication. Whether connecting with a colleague on another continent or engaging in a team discussion, you'll learn to communicate as a mindful, empathetic, and adaptable leader in any setting.

Chapter 9

DIGITAL COMMUNICATION:
THE NEW FRONTIER IN A FAST, PACED WORLD

"The medium is the message."

—Marshall McLuhan.

Imagine sending a quick text to a friend, only to find out later that they misinterpreted your tone as dismissive. Or think back to the last email you received that was so brief it came across as cold or rude. In today's digital world, the meaning of a message often depends as much on how it's delivered as on the words themselves. Marshall McLuhan's insight, "The medium is the message," reminds us that how we communicate shapes understanding in profound ways.

In today's world, a person's presence on social media, what they choose to share, the platforms they use, and how they connect with others on special occasions like birthdays and festivals reveals much about their personality and values. That reminds me of how we used to write postcards to convey wishes and know about other people's well-being in our childhood. Reflecting on the past, we remember when postcards, greeting cards, and letters held immense significance; now, they're nearly extinct in our digital age. Examining how human communication has evolved from these early forms to the present day offers a rich area for research, uncovering insights into our shifting social habits and expressions.

Digital communication has made it easier than ever to connect instantly, share ideas, and build relationships across distances and cultures. Yet this new frontier comes with unique challenges. With Non-verbal cues like body language and tone often absent, it's easy for a message's intent to be misinterpreted. And in a world where miscommunication can happen with just the click of a button, navigating this fast-paced environment requires a conscious approach.

In this chapter, we explore how digital communication has redefined interaction, its benefits and challenges, and ways to communicate mindfully in an era of rapid exchange.

The Double-Edged Sword of Digital Convenience

Digital communication has become an integral part of modern life. From emails and instant messaging to social media and video calls, many conversations now take place through screens. This shift has made staying connected easier but has also brought specific challenges.

Non-verbal cues are often missing without physical presence, affecting how messages are interpreted. For instance, a joke in a text might come across as criticism or a quick email may seem cold or dismissive. With the convenience of instant communication comes the need to be more mindful of tone, word choice, and context.

Misinterpreted Tone in Email Communication

A manager once emailed a team member with a simple "Please see me" regarding a project. Without any further context, the team members spent hours feeling anxious, thinking they were in trouble. In reality, the manager wanted to discuss project updates. Adding words like, "Excited to go over your ideas!" would have changed the interpretation entirely.

Decoding Messages: The Challenge of Tone and Time

One of the biggest hurdles in digital communication is interpreting tone. Even simple phrases can be misread without vocal inflections, body language, or facial expressions. Consider responding with a short "Sure" to a request. While you might mean it positively, it could be indifferent or dismissive. The reader often infers tone from the text, which can lead to misunderstandings. To address this, digital communicators need to practise clear and thoughtful language. Think of the difference between "I'll handle it" and "I'll handle it, don't worry!" While both statements express willingness, adding a reassuring phrase and emoji creates a warmer tone, reducing potential ambiguity.

I remember sending a brief, 'Got it' response to a friend after a long text they sent. While I intended it as acknowledgment, they took it as dismissive, feeling I wasn't interested in their thoughts. This slight misunderstanding reminded me how even simple responses can be misconstrued without tone or context. I have also seen people misinterpreting delayed responses, feeling hurt and unimportant just because I responded a few minutes late.

The Impact of Information Overload

In the digital era, we are constantly bombarded with information emails, texts, notifications, social media posts, and news alerts. According to a study by the International Data Corporation (IDC), the average person spends six to seven hours daily consuming digital content. This nonstop flow can dilute attention, making it challenging to retain essential details and prioritise conversations.

Psychologist Gloria Mark's research at the University of California suggests that refocusing takes around 23 minutes after an interruption, illustrating how multitasking in digital environments can fragment our attention.

I used to keep notifications on for every app, feeling the need to stay constantly updated. But I was distracted and drained, missing out on focused time with my family or projects. Limiting notifications and prioritising information transformed my focus and peace of mind. I now have all my notifications on mute. I check the phone, specific apps, and social media when needed or when I have time. Consider setting a goal to streamline your notifications or set dedicated times to check your messages. Observing the effect on your focus and mental clarity could help you prioritise meaningful interactions.

Shaping Behaviour: The Psychology of Digital Design

The digital environment isn't just a neutral space; it's actively designed to shape behaviour. Social media platforms, for example, use algorithms to promote content based on likes, shares, and comments, encouraging instant reactions and quick judgments. This constant push for engagement shapes not only individual behaviour but also collective communication patterns, influencing how we respond to news and interact socially online. Instagram, for instance, sends notifications based on engagement algorithms, leading users to check their app frequently. Recognising this design can help users consciously reduce impulse reactions and focus on purposeful engagement.

Practical Tips for Digital Mindfulness

Given the complexities of digital communication, approaching it mindfully can help reduce misunderstandings and improve connections.

- **Practise Digital Etiquette**

  Digital communication has its own etiquette principles that help maintain clarity and empathy:

  - *Be Clear and Precise:* Avoid ambiguity and be as specific as possible, especially when making requests or giving feedback.

  - *State Emotions Clearly:* Text can lack emotional nuance. If you're excited or concerned, say it openly to prevent misinterpretation.

  - *Thoughtful Emoji Use:* Emoji can add warmth in casual interactions but may be inappropriate in formal contexts.

- **Prioritise Emotional Clarity**

  Adding emotional clarity to digital messages can reduce ambiguity. Instead of sending a brief, potentially concerning message like "We need to talk," add context: "I'm concerned about our project deadline and would like to discuss solutions."

Case Study on Emotional Clarity

In a remote work scenario, a team member sends a Slack message saying, "Let's connect about the report." The recipient feels apprehensive, thinking they've made a mistake. Had the sender added, "Great work so far; I have some ideas to discuss," the message would have been received with less anxiety.

The Future of Digital Interaction: Moving Beyond Speed

As digital communication continues to evolve, mastering it will be a key skill for personal and professional success. Emerging technologies like virtual and augmented reality may one day bridge some gaps left by text-only communication, adding new dimensions to how we connect. As these tools develop, the most successful communicators will be those who balance the convenience of speed with an emphasis on quality, depth, and intention.

Summary

Digital communication has reshaped how we connect and interact, making it easy to stay in touch and introducing unique challenges. Without Non-verbal cues like body language and tone, digital messages are often open to interpretation, leading to misunderstandings. This chapter explored the complexities of digital communication, from interpreting tone in text messages to managing the psychological impact of information overload. By being mindful of tone, curating content, and recognising how digital platforms shape behaviour, we can navigate this fast-paced world with intentionality and empathy. Practising digital mindfulness enables us to communicate with clarity, maintain focus, and foster meaningful connections, even in a screen-mediated world.

Key Takeaways

- **Recognise the Double-Edged Nature of Digital Communication**: The convenience of digital communication requires heightened awareness of tone, context, and clarity.

- **Decoding Tone and Emotional Nuance**: Interpreting and conveying tone effectively in text-based communication prevents misunderstandings.

- **Manage Information Overload**: Practising digital minimalism, such as limiting notifications and curating content, can reduce stress and improve focus.

- **Awareness of Design Influence**: Recognising how digital platforms shape behaviour enables intentional, balanced engagement.

- **Commit to Mindful Habits**: Approaching digital interactions with patience, empathy, and clarity fosters stronger connections.

Self-Reflection Questions

1. When was the last time a digital message you sent was misunderstood? What could have clarified your tone?

2. How much of your daily digital intake is essential, and what could be streamlined?

3. Are there digital behaviours you'd like to adjust for greater mindfulness?

Self-Assessment Checklist

Rate yourself from 0 to 5 on each point, with 0 being "Never" and 5 being "Always."

1. I ensure my text-based messages convey my intended tone clearly, avoiding ambiguity or unintended harshness. ___/5

2. I pause to consider my response, especially when emotions are involved, rather than reacting impulsively. ___/5

3. I consciously choose the content I consume online, limiting distractions and notifications to prioritise information aligned with my goals and values. ___/5

4. In digital conversations, I approach others with empathy and respect, remembering there's a person behind each message. ___/5

5. I recognise when digital platforms (like social media algorithms) shape my behaviour and take steps to manage my digital habits intentionally. ___/5

Chapter 10

ADAPTING COMMUNICATION ACROSS CULTURES

"Culture is the widening of the mind and of the spirit."

—Jawaharlal Nehru

Picture yourself at an international conference, engaging with colleagues from across the globe. Each handshake, smile, and word exchanged carries nuances rooted in unique cultural norms. What might seem like a straightforward conversation to you could be laden with layers of meaning for someone from a different cultural background. A simple gesture, tone, or word choice can bridge divides or create unintentional misunderstandings.

As Jawaharlal Nehru's words remind us, culture is not merely a collection of customs; it is the lens through which we view and engage with the world. It shapes how we think, feel, and, most importantly, communicate. In today's interconnected world, where virtual meetings and global collaborations are routine, the ability to adapt our communication to diverse cultural contexts has become not just a valuable skill but an essential one.

Globalisation has brought people closer than ever, enabling unprecedented opportunities for collaboration and connection. Yet, these opportunities come with the challenge of understanding the deeply ingrained communication styles and expectations that vary across cultures. For instance, a straightforward email in one culture may be perceived as abrupt in another, and silence might signify contemplation in one setting but disapproval in another.

In this chapter, we delve into the fascinating world of cross-cultural communication. We will explore how cultural nuances influence communication styles, their challenges, and practical strategies for navigating these differences to foster mutual respect, understanding, and meaningful connections. Whether in a boardroom, a classroom, or a casual conversation, mastering the art of cultural adaptability will transform how we relate to others and broaden our perspective of the world.

Understanding Cultural Nuances in Communication

Effective communication goes beyond language; it encompasses values, beliefs, and unspoken cultural norms. Anthropologist Edward T. Hall's framework of high-context and low-context communication offers a valuable perspective on these differences. Importantly, the terms "high" and "low" do not imply a hierarchy, superiority, or inferiority between cultures. They merely describe different approaches to conveying meaning.

Both styles are equally valid and reflect the unique values and social dynamics of the cultures they originate from. Understanding this spectrum is not about determining which style is better but about appreciating the diversity in how people communicate and finding ways to bridge these differences with respect and empathy.

High-Context Cultures

Communication is often nuanced, layered, and implied in high-context cultures, such as Japan, India, and parts of the Middle East. Much of the meaning is derived from Non-verbal cues, shared history, and situational context. Words alone may not carry the entire message; people rely on tone, body language, and established relationships to interpret meaning.

Low-Context Cultures

In contrast, low-context cultures, like those in the United States, Germany, and Northern Europe, tend to favour explicit, straightforward communication. Clarity and precision are highly valued, with a focus on minimising ambiguity to avoid misunderstandings. In these settings, words carry the primary message, and Non-verbal cues are less critical.

Understanding these dimensions helps us appreciate that communication styles are not "better" or "worse" across cultures; they reflect different values and social norms. Learning to navigate this spectrum can help us approach cross, cultural communication with more openness and empathy, avoiding assumptions or stereotypes.

Business Meeting

Imagine an American executive (from a low-context culture) meeting with a Japanese team (from a high-context culture) to discuss a business partnership. The American executive outlines the project expectations and deadlines in detail. The Japanese team members listen attentively, nod politely, and avoid direct questions. The American executive interprets this as agreement and believes the project is moving forward.

However, in Japanese culture, disagreement or critique, especially in a formal setting, may be implied rather than stated openly. In this case, the Japanese team's silence and politeness are signs of respect, but the American executive misreads them as approval.

This example shows the importance of understanding high-context communication norms, where indirect responses may mask deeper concerns that could emerge in a private conversation.

The Art of Saying "No" in India vs Germany

In India, saying "no" directly is often considered too blunt, so it's often softened with phrases like "I'll try" or "It could be challenging" to imply disagreement without outright refusal. This may be indecisive or ambiguous for a German manager (from a low, context culture) who is used to straightforward responses.

In contrast, Germans value directness and clarity, which they see as respectful of others' time. A German might say "no" if something isn't feasible, without intending offence. To an Indian counterpart, however, this may feel abrupt or even disrespectful.

Navigating High and Low-Context Communication in a Multinational Team

A multinational company in the United States organises a virtual meeting with teams from the US, South Korea, and Italy to gather feedback on a product launch.

- The US team (low, context culture) prefers clear, concise feedback presented in a structured, bullet-point format.

- The South Korean team (high, context culture) values group harmony and indirect communication, preferring to give subtle feedback to avoid confrontation.

- The Italian team uses a mix of directness and context and engages in lively discussions, balancing expressiveness with respect for hierarchy.

The US team presents a detailed timeline during the meeting and asks for feedback. The South Korean team members offer supportive phrases but avoid direct concerns, expecting any severe issues to be discussed privately. The Italian team raises a few points openly, seeing this as a collaborative problem-solving. Later, it became apparent that the South Korean team had some timeline concerns, but these were not voiced directly.

To bridge these communication differences, the project manager encourages each team to submit written feedback after each meeting, giving those from high-context cultures space to share their perspectives. Private follow-up discussions also allow for open dialogue, bridging gaps between high and low context preferences. The result is a more inclusive and collaborative environment, illustrating the importance of adapting communication to diverse cultural expectations.

The Role of Non-verbal Communication across Cultures

Non-verbal communication, including body language, gestures, and facial expressions, also varies widely across cultures, shaping how messages are conveyed and interpreted.

Eye Contact: In Western cultures, such as the United States, eye contact signifies attentiveness, respect, and honesty. However, in many Asian cultures, including parts of India, prolonged eye contact with elders or authority figures may be viewed as disrespectful or confrontational.

Gestures: Simple hand gestures can carry vastly different meanings across cultures. For example, while a thumbs-up is a positive sign in many Western countries, it can also be offensive in parts of the Middle East. In India, the "Namaste" gesture is a respectful greeting, with palms pressed together, whereas a handshake might be preferred in Western settings.

Personal Space and Touch: Proxemics, or personal space, differs significantly across cultures. In Latin American and Mediterranean regions, proximity is often acceptable during conversations, while people in Northern Europe or Japan may prefer more personal space. Understanding comfort levels with gestures like handshakes versus the Indian "Namaste" can help navigate social boundaries respectfully.

By recognising these Non-verbal cues and respecting cultural norms, we can convey empathy and awareness in our interactions.

Adapting Verbal Communication across Cultures

Effective cross-cultural communication also involves recognising different verbal styles, from the directness of low-context cultures to the subtlety of high-context cultures.

Direct vs. Indirect Communication

Clearance and assertiveness are valued in direct cultures like the US and Germany, with feedback often given directly. Meanwhile, preserving harmony and "saving face" is important in cultures like Japan and India, leading to more nuanced communication with implied meanings.

Reflect on when someone's pauses or choice of words shaped a conversation. In cross-cultural settings, consider what is said and what remains unsaid; indirect cues often carry significant meaning.

Formality and Politeness

In countries like Japan and South Korea, strict norms of formality and respect apply, especially when addressing elders or authority figures. Western cultures like the US tend to be more casual, even in professional settings. Being aware of these cultural expectations can help avoid unintended offence.

Practical Strategies for Effective Cross-Cultural Communication

Effective cross-cultural communication requires flexibility, awareness, and a genuine openness to learning. Here are some ways to navigate cultural differences:

- *Cultivate Cultural Awareness*: Learn the norms and values of the cultures you interact with. Understanding basics like high-context and low-context preferences can help prevent misunderstandings and build goodwill.

- *Practise Active Listening*: Listening attentively, focusing on spoken and unspoken cues, showing respect, and enhancing communication. Patience and openness signal attentiveness and help you pick up on deeper meanings.

- *Check Your Assumptions*: All cultural assumptions shape our interactions. Stay open-minded and avoid judging other communication styles based on your cultural norms.

- *Ask for Clarification*: When you're unsure, don't hesitate to ask. Seeking clarification is often more effective than making assumptions.

- *Adapt Your Communication Style*: Adjusting your approach based on the cultural context shows respect and adaptability. A softer tone might be more effective for indirect cultures, while direct cultures appreciate clarity and precision.

A Cross-Cultural Communication Lesson

Imagine managing a team with colleagues from Japan, the US, and India. During a group meeting, the Japanese team members remain quiet, the US team members openly share opinions, and the Indian team members nod in agreement but avoid direct critique.

You may initially interpret the Japanese and Indian team members' silence as agreement, but in these cultures, silence can indicate consideration or hesitation. To ensure everyone's perspective is heard, you arrange individual follow, ups, creating a space for open feedback.

This small adjustment fosters collaboration and inclusion, strengthening the team's effectiveness.

Cultural Influence on Digital Communication

Cultural nuances are amplified in digital interactions due to the lack of physical presence. High-context communicators may use fewer words, relying on context, leading to misunderstandings with low-context communicators who prefer explicit instructions.

For instance, an American colleague may expect a direct email with clear action points, while a Japanese colleague may interpret the same email differently, expecting implied instructions. Being mindful of these differences can help prevent miscommunication in digital environments.

Cultural diversity enriches communication, offering learning, adapting, and growing opportunities. By understanding cultural nuances, practising empathy, and adapting our approach, we can bridge divides and foster deeper connections in an increasingly globalised world. Remember, effective cross-cultural communication isn't about abandoning one's style but about recognising and respecting the unique perspectives others bring to the table.

Summary

The chapter delves into the importance of adapting communication styles to effectively navigate cultural differences in today's interconnected world. It explores how cultures can differ in their approach to communication, whether direct or indirect, and how these differences impact personal, professional, and social interactions. Using Edward T. Hall's framework of high, context, and low-context cultures, the chapter explains the importance of understanding subtle nuances in communication, such as indirect communication in high-context cultures like Japan and India, versus the straightforward approach in low, context cultures like the United States and Germany. By providing real-life examples of miscommunications in cross, cultural settings, such as business meetings and team collaborations, this chapter illustrates the need for empathy, awareness, and adaptability in multicultural environments. Practical strategies are shared to help readers improve cross, cultural interactions, including cultivating cultural awareness, practising active listening, and adapting communication styles to suit cultural preferences. The chapter emphasizes that effective cross, cultural communication involves more than just understanding language, it requires an appreciation for the values and norms that shape how people interact.

Key Takeaways

1. **Cultural Differences in Communication Styles**: Understanding high, context and low, context cultures is essential for effective communication. High, context cultures, like Japan and India, often rely on implied meanings, while low, context cultures, such as the United States and Germany, prefer explicit and direct communication.

2. **Non-verbal Communication Varies Across Cultures**: Elements like eye contact, gestures, and personal space have different meanings depending on the culture. Recognizing these differences helps avoid misinterpretations and promotes respectful communication.

3. **Navigating High, and Low, Context Cultures**: Adapting your communication approach based on the context can prevent misunderstandings. High, context cultures may appreciate subtlety and indirect feedback, while low, context cultures value directness and precision.

4. **Practical Strategies for Effective Cross, Cultural Communication**: Cultivate cultural awareness, practice active listening, and be open to adjusting your communication style based on cultural norms. This helps build trust and clarity in multicultural environments.

5. **The Role of Digital Communication**: Cultural nuances also influence digital communication. Being mindful of communication preferences in written interactions is key to preventing misunderstandings in a diverse, global environment.

Reflection

To deepen your understanding of cross, cultural communication, consider these questions:

- Think of a past cross, cultural conversation. Did you notice any unspoken cues or differences in communication style?

- What assumptions did you bring to the conversation? How might they have influenced the interaction?

- How can you incorporate flexibility in your communication to accommodate different cultural expectations in the future?

Self-Assessment Checklist

Rate yourself from 0 to 5 on each point, with 0 being "Never" and 5 being "Always."

1. I ensure my text-based messages convey my intended tone clearly, avoiding ambiguity or unintended harshness. ___ / 5

2. I pause to consider my response, especially when emotions are involved, rather than reacting impulsively. ___ / 5

3. I consciously choose the content I consume online, limiting distractions and notifications to prioritise information aligned with my goals and values. ___ / 5

4. In digital conversations, I approach others with empathy and respect, remembering there's a person behind each message. ___ / 5

5. I recognise when digital platforms (like social media algorithms) shape my behaviour and take steps to manage my digital habits intentionally. ___ / 5

Chapter 11

EMOTIONAL INTELLIGENCE IN COMMUNICATION

*"No one cares how much you know until
they know how much you care."*

—Theodore Roosevelt

Imagine you're in a meeting, brimming with ideas and data, confident that your presentation will win everyone over. You've prepared extensively, triple-checked your slides, and rehearsed each point perfectly. As you speak, your delivery is seamless, and every detail is accounted for. Yet, as you wrap up and scan the room, the response is far from what you expected blank stares, hesitant nods, and a lingering silence. You ask if there are any questions, but no one speaks up.

Later, a colleague approaches and hesitantly shares some feedback: "Your presentation was thorough, but it felt a little one-sided. You didn't seem open to questions or other perspectives. It felt like you were presenting, not connecting."

This moment offers a valuable lesson in emotional intelligence's subtle, often overlooked power in communication. While facts and expertise are crucial, they only resonate when people feel understood and valued. Your logic was flawless, but what was missing was the human connection, the ability to tune into the room's emotional dynamics, notice the disengaged expressions, and adapt your approach in real time.

As Roosevelt's words remind us, "No one cares how much you know until they know how much you care." Genuine connection stems from showing empathy, understanding, and sensitivity to the emotions of others. Emotional intelligence bridges this gap, helping us transform transactional exchanges into meaningful interactions that leave a lasting impact.

Emotional intelligence (EI) is the bridge between what we say and how it's received. It empowers us to manage our own emotions, understand the feelings of those around us, and adapt our communication to foster trust and connection. Think about the conversations that have left a lasting impact on you. Were they laden with facts and figures, or were they moments where someone truly "got" you, your struggles, aspirations, and feelings?

In this chapter, we'll explore how EI transforms everyday interactions into meaningful connections. We'll uncover how being attuned to emotions, both yours and others', can help you navigate challenges, diffuse conflicts, and inspire trust. Whether in the workplace, at home, or in social settings, mastering emotional intelligence isn't just a skill it's the cornerstone of effective and compassionate communication.

What is Emotional Intelligence?

Emotional intelligence (EI) is the ability to recognise, understand, and manage our own emotions while also perceiving, influencing, and responding effectively to the emotions of others. Psychologists Peter Salovey and John Mayer, who first conceptualised the term, defined EI as a set of skills that enable individuals to perceive, assess, and express emotions accurately. In his seminal work Emotional Intelligence, Daniel Goleman expanded this concept further, identifying five core components of EI: self-awareness, self-regulation, motivation, empathy, and social skills. Together, these dimensions serve as the foundation of emotionally intelligent communication, allowing individuals to connect more deeply, navigate conflicts, and foster mutual understanding.

The Role of Emotional Intelligence in Communication

- *Enhancing Understanding:* EI helps us pick up on subtle emotional cues, allowing us to interpret the feelings behind others' words. Consider a scenario where, during a team meeting, Sam notices Lisa saying, "I'm okay with this project," with a quiet tone and tense body language. Realising she may have concerns, he follows up privately and learns more, thus fostering open communication.

- *Building Trust and Rapport:* Empathy and validation foster trust, making others feel genuinely respected. Sarah shares a personal challenge with her manager, Emily, who listens to her struggle and acknowledges it without jumping to solutions. Sarah feels valued and supported, which strengthens their relationship and creates a positive work environment.

- *Resolving Conflict:* EI enables us to approach conflicts calmly and carefully by managing our emotions. During a disagreement on project priorities, Ahmed uses EI to stay calm and focus on shared goals, encouraging his co-workers to do the same. Together, they find a solution that works for both parties.

- *Strengthening Active Listening:* Emotional intelligence helps us listen beyond words, recognising emotional undertones that deepen conversations. When discussing a client's needs, Tom hears hesitation when they mention deadlines. He asks, "It sounds like timing might be a concern. Could we work on a timeline that feels manageable?" By tuning in, Tom demonstrates that he values their input.

- *Encouraging Constructive Feedback*: EI enables us to deliver sensitive and constructive feedback. Jenna frames her input by saying, "I appreciate the effort you put into this project. Let's look at a few adjustments to make it even better." This approach encourages open dialogue without putting the other person on the defensive.

- *Promoting Self-Awareness*: Self-awareness allows us to monitor our emotions and respond intentionally rather than impulsively. When Chris feels irritated by a delayed project update, he takes a moment to reflect. Instead of snapping, he calmly asks if there are challenges, leading to a more constructive conversation.

- *Fostering Adaptability*: EI enables us to adjust our communication style to suit others' emotional states and personalities. During a client presentation, Maya notices they seem overwhelmed, so she slows down and simplifies her points. This adjustment helps them feel more engaged and comfortable.

- *Increasing Persuasion and Influence*: EI helps us craft messages that resonate on a deeper level. Knowing his team values transparency, Rahul clearly explains a new policy and invites questions. By building trust through openness, he persuades them to support the change.

- *Supporting a Positive Work Culture*: Leaders with high EI create empathetic environments that promote collaboration. In team meetings, Meera recognises individual contributions, fostering a culture of respect. Her style inspires others to support one another and contributes to a positive work atmosphere.

- *Building Resilience in Communication*: EI helps us manage stress during difficult conversations, keeping us composed. During a tense negotiation, Daniel remains calm and focuses on shared goals. His steady demeanour helps keep the conversation productive and prevents escalation.

The Core Components of Emotional Intelligence

The concept of Emotional Intelligence (EI) was first explored by psychologists Peter Salovey and John Mayer, who described it as the ability to perceive, understand, and regulate emotions effectively. Daniel Goleman later popularised EI in his book *Emotional Intelligence: Why It Can Matter More Than IQ*, where he identified five core components: self-awareness, self-regulation, motivation, empathy, and social skills. These elements are essential for navigating complex interpersonal dynamics, fostering deeper connections, and enhancing communication across personal and professional contexts. Research published in *Harvard Business Review* suggests that EI is a key predictor of success, particularly in leadership roles because it enhances collaboration, conflict resolution, and adaptability.

Let's delve into these components with real-world examples to understand their relevance:

1. **Self-Awareness: Understanding Your Emotions**

Self-awareness is the ability to recognise and understand one's emotions and how they affect one's behaviour and interactions. It forms the foundation of EI, enabling individuals to make thoughtful decisions rather than being driven solely by emotional impulses.

Imagine you're preparing for an important presentation and feeling anxious. Self-aware individuals might acknowledge, "I'm feeling nervous because I care deeply about this project." By identifying the emotion, they can take proactive steps, such as practising their speech or using calming techniques, to manage it effectively.

2. **Self-Regulation: Managing Emotional Responses**

Self-regulation involves controlling impulsive reactions, staying calm under pressure, and responding thoughtfully rather than reactively. This skill is crucial for maintaining professionalism and fostering trust.

In a heated team meeting, someone criticises your work unfairly. Instead of lashing out, self-regulation helps you pause, take a deep breath, and respond, "I understand your concerns. Let's discuss this further to find a resolution." This measured response shifts the focus from conflict to collaboration.

3. Motivation: Driving Inner Excellence

Motivation in EI refers to the internal drive to achieve goals, stay resilient in the face of challenges, and find fulfilment beyond external rewards. Motivated individuals often inspire those around them through their passion and dedication.

A project leader faces a major setback when a client rejects their proposal. Instead of feeling defeated, their motivation pushes them to rework the idea with renewed energy, inspiring their team to persist. This attitude fosters creativity and resilience, encouraging others to stay committed to the shared goal.

4. Empathy: Understanding and Sharing the Feelings of Others

Empathy is the ability to understand and share the emotions of others. It allows you to see situations from another person's perspective, building trust and deepening connections. If a colleague appears unusually quiet during a meeting, an empathetic individual might approach them afterward and ask, "You seemed a bit distracted today. Is everything okay?" This simple act of care can create an opportunity for support and understanding, strengthening workplace relationships.

5. Social Skills: Building Strong Interpersonal Relationships

Social skills encompass effective communication, conflict resolution, and influencing and inspiring others. They are vital for fostering collaboration, resolving disputes, and creating harmonious environments.

During a team project, one member dominates discussions, leaving others feeling unheard. A socially skilled leader might address this by saying, "Let's ensure everyone has a chance to share their thoughts. I'd love to hear your perspectives." This approach encourages inclusivity and fosters a collaborative team dynamic.

By mastering these five components, individuals can enhance their emotional intelligence and significantly improve their ability to communicate, connect, and lead effectively. These skills shape personal interactions and play a pivotal role in professional growth and success.

Expanding the Role of Emotional Intelligence in Digital Communication

In an increasingly digital world, the principles of Emotional Intelligence (EI) are not just relevant, they're essential. As communication shifts to emails, text messages, and social media platforms, the absence of physical and Non-verbal cues can make interactions prone to misunderstandings. Here's how EI becomes a cornerstone for navigating these challenges:

1. **Interpreting Textual Tone**

Written messages often lack the vocal inflections and body language that help convey intent. Without these cues, recipients may misinterpret tone, potentially leading to confusion or conflict. EI equips us to read between the lines, discern emotional undertones, and seek clarity when needed.

Example: Imagine receiving an email that reads, "This needs to be fixed ASAP." Without context, the tone might feel abrupt or accusatory. Instead of reacting defensively, EI encourages you to consider possible scenarios: Is the sender stressed? Is there an urgent deadline? Responding with empathy, "I understand the urgency and will prioritise this," can defuse tension and foster collaboration.

2. Managing Impulsive Reactions

The immediacy of digital platforms often tempts us to react impulsively, especially in emotionally charged situations. EI encourages pausing to reflect before responding, ensuring our words are measured and constructive rather than reactive.

Example: A social media comment unfairly criticises your work. Instead of retaliating, EI prompts you to take a moment to breathe, assess the feedback objectively, and respond with grace: "Thank you for your input. I'd love to hear more about your perspective on improving." This thoughtful approach maintains professionalism and shifts the conversation toward productive dialogue.

3. Building Online Rapport

Empathy is the cornerstone of building meaningful connections, even in digital spaces. Acknowledging others' emotions, validating their experiences, and responding with understanding can bridge gaps created by the lack of physical presence.

Example: In a virtual team meeting, a colleague might appear disengaged. Instead of assuming disinterest, an emotionally intelligent response might involve reaching out privately: "I noticed you seemed quiet today. Are you feeling overwhelmed? Let me know how I can support you." This simple gesture fosters trust and strengthens relationships, even across screens.

4. Fostering Clarity and Connection in Written Communication

Clarity becomes even more crucial in digital communication. EI encourages using clear, concise language while incorporating emotional context to ensure messages are understood and relatable.

Example: Instead of sending a vague message like "Let's talk," which might cause unnecessary anxiety, EI suggests providing context: "I'd like to discuss some ideas about our upcoming project. When would be a good time to connect?" This reduces ambiguity, setting a positive tone for the conversation.

5. **Adapting to Digital Norms with Empathy**

Different digital platforms have their etiquette and expectations. EI enables us to adapt while maintaining authenticity and emotional awareness. For example, a professional email might require a formal tone, while a text message to a friend allows casual language and emoji to convey warmth.

The Relevance of EI in a Digital World

Research in digital communication highlights that a lack of context and emotional cues often causes misinterpretations in emails and texts. Studies published in *Psychology Today* emphasise the role of emotional intelligence in mitigating these issues, demonstrating that individuals with high EI are better at maintaining positive relationships and avoiding digital misunderstandings.

By applying EI in digital communication, we can navigate the complexities of tone, intent, and connection, making our interactions more meaningful and effective in a fast-paced, virtual world. Whether it's a thoughtful pause before responding, crafting a message with empathy, or recognising when to clarify intent, EI transforms digital exchanges into opportunities for deeper understanding and collaboration.

Practical Tips for Cultivating Emotional Intelligence in Communication

1.   Engage in Mindfulness

Mindfulness is a foundational practice for developing emotional awareness. By staying present in the moment, you can observe your emotions and reactions without judgment. This helps you recognise emotional triggers and respond thoughtfully instead of impulsively. Imagine feeling frustrated during a tense meeting. Instead of snapping at a colleague, a mindful pause allows you to identify your frustration and refocus on constructive dialogue. This not only preserves professionalism but also fosters mutual respect.

Quick Tip: To strengthen your emotional self-awareness, incorporate short mindfulness exercises into your routine, such as deep breathing or a two-minute focus on sensations.

2.   Seek Constructive Feedback

Feedback is a valuable tool for uncovering blind spots in your emotional intelligence. By inviting input from trusted colleagues, friends, or mentors, you can identify areas for growth and adjust your communication style to be more effective.

A friend might point out that your habit of unintentionally interrupting during conversations comes across as dismissive. With this awareness, you can practice active listening, ensuring others feel heard and respected.

Quick Tip: Ask specific questions like, "Do you feel I listen actively during discussions?" or "How could I improve the tone of my messages?" This encourages actionable feedback.

3. Express Emotions Clearly

Clear expression of emotions is vital to building trust and understanding in communication. Instead of masking or minimising feelings, name them directly to provide clarity and authenticity.

Instead of saying "I'm fine" when feeling overwhelmed, try "I'm feeling a bit stressed about the deadline and could use some support." This invites empathy and enables others to respond meaningfully.

Quick Tip: Practice using "I" statements to articulate emotions: "I feel [emotion] because [reason]." This approach keeps communication non-confrontational and clear.

4. Practice Empathetic Listening

Empathy is at the heart of emotional intelligence. Listening with empathy involves giving your full attention, acknowledging the other person's emotions, and responding with care. If a colleague shares frustration about a project, avoid dismissing their concerns with "It'll work out." Instead, respond with, "I understand how that could be frustrating. How can I help?" This validates their emotions and fosters collaboration.

Quick Tip: Paraphrase what the other person says to show understanding: "It sounds like you're feeling [emotion] because of [reason]. Did I get that right?"

5. Reflect on Your Interactions

Post-conversation reflection helps identify moments where you succeeded in demonstrating emotional intelligence and areas for improvement.

After a meeting, you might realise your tone was overly firm. Reflecting on this allows you to adjust your approach in future interactions, such as softening your tone or incorporating more positive language.

Quick Tip: Keep a journal of challenging interactions and reflect on how you handled them. Note what went well and what you could do differently next time.

6. Adapt Communication to Context

Different situations and people require different approaches. Tailor your tone, words, and gestures to align with the emotional needs of the interaction.

In a feedback session, balancing honesty with empathy ensures the recipient feels supported rather than criticised. "I value your effort, and I think we can make this even stronger by focusing on [specific area]" conveys both encouragement and constructive guidance.

Quick Tip: Before important conversations, consider the other person's perspective and emotional state. Adjust your approach accordingly to create a positive impact.

Cultural Dimensions of Emotional Intelligence

Emotional intelligence transcends individual interactions, playing a crucial role in navigating the complexities of cross-cultural communication. Culture profoundly influences how emotions are expressed, perceived, and managed, making it essential to develop a culturally sensitive approach to EI. Emotional expressions that are natural in one culture might be misunderstood or even offensive in another. Cultivating EI across cultural boundaries ensures that communication remains respectful, empathetic, and effective.

Geert Hofstede's cultural dimensions theory provides valuable insight into how culture influences emotional dynamics. Dimensions such as individualism vs collectivism, power distance, uncertainty avoidance, and long-term orientation highlight fundamental differences in how cultures approach relationships, emotions, and authority. Applying these insights to emotional intelligence allows individuals to adapt their communication styles, fostering understanding and reducing conflict.

Adapting Emotional Intelligence across Cultures

A global team of members from the United States, India, and Japan faced challenges during a virtual project discussion. The American members (low-context, individualistic) expressed their concerns directly, while the Indian members (high-context, collectivistic) preferred subtle hints. The Japanese members (high-context, collectivistic) remained silent to avoid confrontation.

- **Challenge**: The Americans' directness was perceived as aggressive, while the Indians' subtlety and the Japanese's silence were interpreted as agreement.

- **Solution**: The team leader used emotional intelligence to bridge the gap by creating a safe space for feedback, encouraging written input for the Japanese team, and balancing direct and indirect communication styles. This approach fostered collaboration, ensuring all voices were heard and respected.

Practical Tips for Culturally Sensitive EI

1. **Learn About Cultures**: Study the cultural backgrounds of those you interact with to anticipate emotional preferences.

2. **Ask, Don't Assume**: Ask for clarification rather than relying on assumptions when in doubt.

3. **Adapt Flexibly**: Be willing to adjust your emotional expression and tone based on cultural norms.

4. **Seek Feedback**: Request input from colleagues or friends on how your communication style aligns with their cultural expectations.

Culturally sensitive emotional intelligence is the key to navigating a globalised world. By recognising cultural influences on emotions and adapting communication accordingly, we can build stronger relationships, resolve conflicts effectively, and foster mutual respect. As Daniel Goleman emphasised in *Emotional Intelligence*, EI is not a fixed trait but a skill that evolves with practice, especially in multicultural settings. Individuals can connect authentically and meaningfully across cultural divides by cultivating this skill.

Importance of Non-verbal Emotional Cues

Non-verbal emotional cues, such as facial expressions, body language, and tone of voice, play a crucial role in emotional intelligence (EI), shaping how emotions are conveyed and interpreted. Psychologist Albert Mehrabian's research revealed that up to 93% of communication effectiveness comes from Non-verbal elements like tone (38%) and body language (55%), emphasising their impact on emotional understanding. These cues provide context that words alone often cannot, allowing individuals to interpret feelings, intentions, and attitudes accurately.

In hybrid settings like video calls, the importance of Non-verbal cues becomes even more pronounced. While physical presence is limited, maintaining eye contact with the camera, using open gestures, and modulating tone can convey empathy and engagement. A study published in the *Journal of Business and Psychology* (2021) found that video communication enriched with intentional Non-verbal behaviours, such as smiling or nodding, significantly enhanced trust and rapport in virtual teams.

Recognising and adapting Non-verbal signals in communication fosters emotional awareness, ensuring messages resonate authentically. Whether in face-to-face or hybrid environments, these cues remain integral to building trust, reducing miscommunication, and creating emotionally intelligent interactions.

Summary

The chapter "Emotional Intelligence in Communication" examined the pivotal role of Emotional Intelligence (EI) in fostering meaningful and effective interactions. It emphasised that EI bridges the gap between what is said and how it is perceived, as Theodore Roosevelt's quote, "No one cares how much you know until they know how much you care," aptly illustrates. The chapter explored EI's core components self-awareness, self-regulation, motivation, empathy, and social skills and their transformative impact on communication.

The discussion extended to EI's role in resolving conflicts, building trust, encouraging active listening, and fostering adaptability. It highlighted the importance of Non-verbal emotional cues, such as tone, body language, and facial expressions, in conveying empathy and understanding, even in hybrid settings like video calls. Additionally, the chapter introduced the concept of culturally sensitive EI, addressing how emotional expressions and interpretations vary across cultures and emphasising the need for awareness and adaptability to navigate multicultural interactions effectively.

Key Takeaways

1. **Core Components of EI**: Developing self-awareness, self-regulation, motivation, empathy, and social skills enhances communication effectiveness and fosters meaningful connections.

2. **Resolving Conflicts**: EI allows for calm, empathetic conflict resolution, focusing on shared goals and mutual understanding.

3. **Active Listening**: EI deepens listening skills by recognising and responding to emotional undertones in conversations.

4. **Adaptability in Communication**: Tailoring communication styles to others' emotional needs and cultural contexts strengthens rapport and inclusivity.

5. **Importance of Non-verbal Cues**: Non-verbal signals, such as facial expressions, body language, and tone, provide critical context and emotional depth in interactions, particularly in hybrid and digital settings.

6. **Culturally Sensitive EI**: Understanding how cultural norms influence emotional expressions and interpretations fosters respect and connection in diverse environments.

Reflection Activities

1. Reflect on a recent conversation where Non-verbal cues (e.g., tone or body language) played a significant role in shaping your understanding. What did these signals convey, and how did they influence your response?

2. Consider a time when cultural differences affected an interaction. How did you adapt, or how could you have approached the situation more empathetically and effectively?

3. Think about how you use emotional intelligence in digital or hybrid settings, such as video calls. Are you intentional about maintaining eye contact, using open gestures, and modulating your tone to convey empathy and engagement?

Self-Assessment Checklist

Rate each statement from 0 (Rarely) to 5 (Consistently):

1. I recognise and understand my emotions during interactions and their impact on my responses. ___ / 5

2. I practise self-regulation by managing my emotional reactions, especially in difficult or high-pressure situations. ___ / 5

3. I actively listen to others, acknowledge their emotions, and demonstrate empathy. ___ / 5

4. I provide constructive feedback sensitive to others' feelings and perspectives. ___ / 5

5. I adjust my tone, language, and approach to align with each conversation's emotional and situational needs. ___ / 5

Chapter 12

THE ART OF STORYTELLING: CRAFTING CONNECTION THROUGH WORDS

"The most powerful person in the world is the storyteller."

—Steve Jobs

Storytelling is more than a way to share ideas. It is how humans connect. As Steve Jobs emphasized, storytellers hold unparalleled influence because they shape perspectives, spark emotions, and drive action. Stories aren't just words strung together; they are bridges that link our experiences, values, and aspirations, fostering understanding and unity.

The Universal Power of Stories

Stories have an extraordinary ability to resonate with us because they mirror the human journey. They reflect our challenges, joys, and hopes, offering a space for empathy and connection. A research reveals that storytelling can enhance emotional engagement and memory, making messages more impactful than facts or statistics. Stories transform abstract concepts into relatable, memorable experiences.

Whether a parent shares a childhood memory to teach a lesson or a global leader recounts a pivotal moment to rally support, stories create a shared emotional landscape. They don't just deliver information, evoke feelings, inspire actions, and leave lasting impressions.

Why Stories Matter in Personal and Professional Settings

In today's **digital and interconnected world,** storytelling has emerged as a vital communication skill, offering authenticity and engagement amidst the noise of information overload. Stories resonate because they transcend words; they tap into emotions, create memorable experiences, and foster genuine human connection. Whether in personal or professional contexts, storytelling bridges gaps in understanding, simplifies complexities, and builds lasting bonds.

Personal Settings: Building Intimacy and Trust

In personal life, stories foster intimacy and trust. Sharing meaningful experiences allows others to see the world through your lens, deepening relationships and cultivating empathy. Stories enable us to connect on a human level, where emotions and experiences precede facts and figures.

Example: A friend recounts a childhood memory of overcoming fear during a swimming lesson, drawing parallels to their child's challenges. This personal narrative creates an emotional connection, offering comfort and inspiration in a relatable way.

Professional Contexts: The Superpower of Storytelling

In professional settings, storytelling is a transformative tool for communication in the modern world. It elevates branding, presentations, and leadership by making messages memorable, impactful, and engaging. Stories turn abstract data into compelling narratives, inspire teams, and align diverse audiences with shared goals.

Example: Imagine a CEO addressing their team during a period of uncertainty. Instead of delivering a sterile report on challenges and strategies, they recount the company's early days when a small team overcame adversity with perseverance and innovation. The CEO ties this narrative to the present moment, saying, "Just as we triumphed against the odds back then, we have the creativity and resilience to navigate these challenges today." This approach informs and motivates employees, fostering a sense of shared purpose, belief in the company's vision, and confidence in their collective ability to succeed.

The Timeless Tool of Engagement

Storytelling's relevance spans centuries, proving that its appeal is timeless. In today's fast-paced, distraction-filled world, stories are a powerful tool to grab attention and leave a mark. Whether an educator simplifies a lesson with an analogy, a leader inspires a team with a heartfelt anecdote, or a marketer crafts a brand narrative, stories bring clarity, relatability, and emotional depth to communication.

The Psychology of Stories

Stories hold a unique power over the human mind, not because they deliver information but because they engage our emotions and senses in ways other forms of communication cannot. Stories activate our brains on multiple levels, weaving facts with feelings, logic with emotion, and ideas with experience.

Why Stories Stick: The Neuroscience of Storytelling

Scientific research has shown that stories stimulate the brain more effectively than raw data or facts. Neuroscientists at Princeton University found that when a person listens to a well-told story, their brain activity synchronizes with the storyteller's. This phenomenon, known as "neural coupling," fosters profound emotional understanding and connection.

Moreover, stories activate multiple areas of the brain responsible for language, sensory experience, and emotion. This engagement makes stories not only more relatable but also more memorable. As researchers at Stanford University discovered, people are twenty-two times more likely to remember a fact when it's presented as part of a story.

How Stories Evoke Emotion

1. **Emotional Triggers**: Stories tap into universal human experiences like love, fear, hope, or resilience. These emotions create a bond between the storyteller and the audience, making the message resonate on a personal level.

   - *Example*: A charity appeal sharing the story of one individual impacted by their work often garners more donations than statistics about thousands served.

2. **Cognitive Empathy**: Hearing a story allows us to step into another person's shoes, fostering empathy. This emotional connection can inspire action or change perspectives.

   - *Example*: A team leader sharing their struggle with work-life balance can encourage their team to embrace flexibility and trust.

Key Elements of a Compelling Story

As Robert McKee, the renowned author of *Story: Substance, Structure, Style and the Principles of Screenwriting*, famously said, "Storytelling is the most powerful way to put ideas into the world today." A compelling story resonates with its audience by combining structure, emotion, and authenticity. These elements ensure that the narrative informs, engages, and inspires.

1. **Structure: Beginning, Middle, and End**

A well-structured story creates clarity and flow, ensuring the audience remains engaged from start to finish. The classic three-act structure provides a roadmap:

- *Beginning:* Introduce the setting, characters, and the problem or goal.

- *Middle:* Explore challenges, conflicts, or transformations, creating emotional engagement.

- *End:* Resolve the narrative with a satisfying conclusion, leaving the audience with a clear takeaway.

Example: In a professional setting, a team leader might share this story during a meeting:

- Beginning: *"When we started the project, we faced a major obstacle our primary supplier went out of business."*

- Middle: *"We brainstormed alternatives, contacted new vendors, and streamlined processes to reduce costs."*

- End: *"Ultimately, we delivered the project on time and even came in under budget, proving that adaptability and teamwork can overcome even unexpected challenges."*

2. **Emotional Resonance: Making the Audience Feel Connected**

Emotion is the glue that binds the audience to a story. Neuroscience research supports this idea, showing that stories engaging emotions activate the brain more intensely than facts, making the message more memorable and impactful.

To evoke emotions:

- Use relatable experiences or universal themes like perseverance, love, or overcoming adversity.

- Show, don't tell: Paint vivid pictures with words to immerse the audience in the narrative.

- Use sensory details to trigger empathy or shared experiences. A director might say:

  "I met a child named Maya, whose family couldn't afford school supplies. When we provided her with a backpack and books, the joy in her eyes was indescribable. Today, Maya is a top student in her class and dreams of becoming a doctor. Stories like Maya's remind us why our mission matters."

This evokes empathy and motivates action, making the story unforgettable.

3. Authenticity: The Importance of Being Genuine and Relatable

Authenticity builds trust. Audiences can sense when a story is genuine versus when it's fabricated or overly polished. Genuine stories create credibility and foster a deeper connection.

Core ideas of authenticity in storytelling:

- Share personal experiences or challenges with vulnerability.

- Avoid exaggeration or over-dramatization, which can undermine trust.

- Tailor the story to the audience's values, showing you understand their perspective.

An entrepreneur might say:

"When I launched my first business, I made countless mistakes. One of the biggest being not listening to my customers. After several failed attempts, I realized that their feedback was invaluable. It wasn't easy to admit my mistakes, but that pivot transformed my approach and led to my first success story."

This story's honesty makes it relatable, inspiring the audience to embrace their own challenges as learning opportunities.

Tying It All Together

A compelling story seamlessly weaves structure, emotion, and authenticity into a narrative that captivates, informs, and inspires. When these elements align, stories become not just tools for communication but transformative experiences that linger in the minds and hearts of the audience.

Types of Stories and Their Impact

Stories come in many forms, each uniquely tailored to achieve specific outcomes. Whether you're building trust, persuading others, or inspiring action, understanding the types of stories and their purpose can amplify your communication impact.

1. **Personal Stories for Connection**

Personal stories draw on authentic experiences, creating relatability and fostering trust. These narratives bridge the gap between speaker and audience, humanizing your message and forging emotional bonds.

- *Purpose:* To build authenticity and emotional connection.

- *Impact:* Personal stories allow your audience to see shared experiences, making your message more engaging and relatable.

  A teacher recounts the time they struggled with a challenging subject in school, emphasizing how perseverance helped them succeed. This resonates with students facing similar hurdles.

A manager shares how their early career mistakes taught them the value of humility and listening, encouraging employees to embrace growth.

2. Professional Stories for Persuasion

Professional stories showcase expertise, problem-solving, and credibility. They are especially effective in presentations, client meetings, or team discussions, where demonstrating impact or aligning perspectives is crucial.

- *Purpose:* To influence decisions, align goals, and demonstrate expertise.

- *Impact:* Professional stories instil confidence in your ideas or solutions by illustrating results and providing evidence of success.

  A marketer explains how a previous campaign increased a client's revenue by 40%, persuading potential clients to adopt a similar strategy.

A team leader narrates how collaboration resolved a significant challenge, inspiring their team to embrace cooperation.

3. Inspirational Stories for Motivation

Inspirational stories ignite hope and determination by showcasing triumph over adversity. These stories are ideal for empowering individuals, sparking action, or rallying collective efforts.

- *Purpose:* To inspire change, encourage resilience, and drive action.

- *Impact:* Inspirational stories leave a lasting emotional impression, motivating the audience to overcome challenges.

  A founder describes starting their organization with a small team and limited resources, eventually growing it into a movement that impacts thousands of lives.

A keynote speaker recounts their journey from failure to success, illustrating how setbacks can become stepping stones.

Examples Illustrating Each Type

Personal Story: *"During my first job interview, I blanked when asked a technical question. It was humbling, but it taught me the value of preparation. Now, I mentor young professionals to help them avoid the same mistakes."*

Professional Story: *"We faced a major crisis when our product launch failed. Instead of giving up, we analysed feedback, pivoted, and launched six months later, doubling our expected sales. This taught our team the importance of resilience and adaptability."*

Inspirational Story: *"Five years ago, I started this initiative with no funding and just one volunteer. We've impacted over a million lives today thanks to belief and hard work. This journey shows that no obstacle is insurmountable if you stay committed to your vision."*

Choosing the Right Story at the Right Time

When selecting a story, consider the audience's needs and the situation:

- Use **personal stories** to build rapport in one-on-one or small group settings.

- Choose **professional stories** to persuade stakeholders, clients, or teams during presentations or meetings.

- Share **inspirational stories** during speeches or moments requiring collective motivation.

By mastering the art of storytelling, you can foster trust, influence decisions, and inspire action, unlocking the full potential of connection through words.

Storytelling Techniques and Strategies

Effective storytelling goes beyond words; it's an art that engages the senses, emotions, and imagination. Using vivid imagery and sensory details helps paint a picture in the listener's mind, making the story memorable and impactful. For example, describing the "crisp autumn air" or the "thrumming excitement in the room" draws the audience into the narrative. Delivery is equally crucial - pauses create suspense, tone conveys emotion, and body language reinforces authenticity, enhancing the story's resonance. Tailoring stories to the audience ensures relevance and connection; a casual anecdote might captivate a close-knit group, while a data-driven narrative may resonate better with professionals. These techniques transform storytelling into a powerful engagement, persuasion, and connection tool.

Practical Applications of Storytelling

In Leadership: Inspiring Teams and Driving Action

Storytelling is a cornerstone of effective leadership. Leaders inspire their teams by sharing stories of vision, success, or overcoming challenges and fostering a shared sense of purpose. For instance, a leader recounting how a team innovatively overcame a tight deadline can motivate others to embrace challenges with creativity and determination.

In Personal Relationships: Building Trust and Understanding

Stories in personal relationships create emotional bonds, deepen understanding, and build trust. Sharing an individual experience, like a moment of vulnerability or a triumph, allows others to connect on a human level. For example, a parent explaining how they overcame fears similar to their child's can provide reassurance and encouragement.

In Presentations: Engaging and Persuading Audiences

Presentations that incorporate storytelling captivate audiences and leave lasting impressions. A well-crafted story can turn complex ideas into relatable concepts and inspire action. For example, a marketer pitching a campaign might share how a similar strategy successfully resonated with consumers, convincing stakeholders of its potential.

By weaving stories into these scenarios, storytelling transforms interactions from transactional to deeply impactful, leaving audiences inspired and connected.

Common Mistakes and How to Avoid Them: Do's and Don'ts

- **Do keep your story concise and focused.**

  Don't overload with unnecessary details that dilute the core message.

- **Do stay authentic and natural in your delivery.**

  Don't rely on a rigid script that makes you sound robotic or insincere.

- **Do consider the audience's needs, interests, and context.**

  Don't forget to tailor your story to resonate with your listeners' perspectives.

- **Do use vivid imagery and relatable examples to engage.**

  Don't rely solely on abstract concepts or jargon that alienates the audience.

- **Do maintain a clear purpose for your story.**

  Don't stray off-topic or lose sight of your message's intent.

Finding Your Storytelling Voice: Discovering your storytelling voice involves aligning your stories with your values, experiences, and authentic self. It's about finding the narratives that matter to you and meaningfully connecting them to your audience.

How to Discover Stories that Resonate

- **Reflect on Pivotal Moments:** Identify significant events or turning points that shaped your values or beliefs.

  Example: A time when overcoming a challenge taught you resilience.

- **Connect to Shared Experiences:** Consider universal themes your audience can relate to, such as growth, perseverance, or connection.

  Example: A lesson learned from a seemingly mundane experience like a missed opportunity or a small victory.

- **Focus on Authenticity:** Choose stories true to your experiences and allow your personality to shine through.

Exercises to Practice Storytelling

1. *Memory Mapping:*

   Write down three impactful moments from your life. For each, note the emotions, lessons, and key takeaways. Practice narrating these stories in 2-3 minutes.

2. *Story Swap:*

   Pair with a friend or colleague and exchange stories on a chosen topic (e.g., a memorable mistake). Share feedback on clarity, engagement, and authenticity.

3. *Record and Review:*

   Record yourself telling a story, then watch it to assess your tone, pacing, and emotional connection. Identify areas for improvement.

4. *The Three-Point Method:*

   Structure your story using:

   - *Beginning:* Set the scene and introduce the context.
   - *Middle:* Present the challenge, conflict, or key event.
   - *End:* Conclude with the resolution and takeaway.

5. *Audience Adaptation:*

   Take a single story and adapt it for three audiences (e.g., a colleague, a friend, and a child). This exercise hones your ability to tailor delivery.

By engaging in these exercises and reflecting on your unique experiences, you'll develop a storytelling voice that feels authentic, purposeful, and impactful. Your stories will resonate with your audience and strengthen your confidence as a storyteller.

Stories That Last a Lifetime

Stories are more than words; they are legacies of connection, learning, and growth. Compelling storytelling can transcend moments, leaving a lasting imprint on the hearts and minds of those who hear them. Stories shape how we relate, inspire, and lead, whether in a heartfelt conversation with a friend, a professional presentation to a team, or a shared anecdote with a child.

We each carry stories worth telling, narratives of perseverance, lessons learned, and dreams pursued. These stories have the potential to teach, heal, and ignite action. Steve Jobs once said, "The most powerful person in the world is the storyteller." By crafting your narratives with intention, emotion, and authenticity, you can wield this power to create meaningful connections and inspire transformation in your life and the lives of others.

The journey of storytelling is ongoing. Start small, reflect on your experiences, and embrace your unique voice. Begin crafting your narratives today because the stories you tell might be the ones that change everything.

Summary

Storytelling is a timeless art that bridges the gap between words and emotions, creating lasting connections in personal and professional settings. From building trust through personal stories to inspiring action with motivational narratives, storytelling transforms communication into a tool for engagement, persuasion, and connection. By mastering the elements of compelling stories, understanding the psychology behind their impact, and practicing techniques like vivid imagery and emotional resonance, anyone can craft narratives that captivate and inspire. Compelling storytelling is about authenticity, purpose, and the ability to adapt stories to different audiences and situations.

Key Takeaways

1. **The Power of Stories**: Stories evoke emotions, create connections, and leave lasting impressions.

2. **Elements of Effective Storytelling**: Structure, emotional resonance, and authenticity are the foundation of compelling narratives.

3. **Types of Stories: Personal, professional, and inspirational stories serve unique purposes, from fostering a** connection to inspiring action.

4. **Storytelling Techniques**: Use vivid imagery, tone, and body language to enhance delivery and tailor stories to the audience.

5. **Practical Applications**: Storytelling is a versatile tool for leadership, personal relationships, and presentations, making communication more impactful.

Reflection Activity

- **Reflect** Recall a story that deeply resonated with you. What made it memorable? Was it the emotions, the delivery, or the message?

- **Identify**: Think of an experience that taught you a powerful lesson. How could you craft it into a story to inspire or connect with others?

- **Practice**: Share this story with a trusted friend or colleague, and ask for feedback on how it made them feel and what they learned.

Self-Assessment Checklist

Rate yourself from 0 (Rarely) to 5 (Consistently):

1. I create stories with a clear structure with beginning, middle, and end. ___ / 5

2. I use vivid imagery and emotions to make my stories engaging. ___ / 5

3. I tailor my stories to resonate with my specific audience. ___ / 5

4. I maintain authenticity and align my stories with my values. ___ / 5

5. I practice storytelling techniques like tone, pauses, and body language for effective delivery. ___ / 5

Part 3: Communication in the Modern World, Situational Skill Building

Instructions: Reflect on the following scenarios, using insights from Part 3 to consider the impact of digital, cultural, and emotional intelligence on communication.

1. *You notice a friend has been distant in your text conversations, giving brief replies. What approach could you take to understand their perspective without making assumptions?*

2. *You need to email feedback on a project to a colleague from another culture. How would you ensure the message is clear, respectful, and considerate of potential cultural differences?*

3. *A colleague seems disengaged and distracted in a video call with your team. How could you address this in a way that respects their feelings and fosters a productive discussion?*

4. *You have noticed you feel misunderstood in group chats with friends. How might you adapt your digital communication style to create clearer, more positive exchanges?*

5. *You manage a team that spans different time zones and communication styles. How can you adjust your approach to respect these differences and maintain a cohesive team environment?*

6. *You're speaking with someone whose first language differs from yours, and they seem to misunderstand some phrases you use. How could you adapt your language and tone to be more inclusive and clear?*

PART 4

COMMUNICATING FOR LASTING IMPACT

*"People will forget what you said, people will forget what you did,
but people will never forget how you made them feel."*

— Maya Angelou.

Communication that lasts goes beyond words; it leaves an imprint on the hearts and minds of others. Part 4 is about stepping into meaningful impact by communicating in ways that inspire, lead, and build legacies. In personal relationships or professional endeavours, impactful communication creates trust, motivates action, and fosters lasting connections.

In this section, you'll explore how to:

- **Lead with Integrity**: Build credibility through authentic, values-driven communication.

- **Harness Storytelling**: Use stories to inspire, connect, and create memorable experiences.

- **Integrate Humour**: Bring lightness to challenging conversations, fostering warmth and approachability.

- **Embrace Lifelong Learning**: Continuously evolve your communication skills to adapt to every stage of life.

This final part ties together the principles you've learned throughout the book, empowering you to use communication for influence, growth, and connection. By mastering these skills, you'll leave a positive, lasting impact on the lives of others; whether you're mentoring a colleague, supporting a loved one, or addressing a room full of people.

As you embark on this concluding segment, remember that impactful communication isn't about perfection but presence, empathy, and intention. Every word, pause, and gesture can potentially shape lives and make a difference.

Are you ready to transform your communication into a legacy of connection, authenticity, and purpose?

Chapter 13

ASSERTIVENESS WITH COMPASSION

"Assertiveness is not what you do; it's who you are."

– Shakti Gawain.

Aabha, a project manager, finds herself in a challenging situation. She is leading a critical project nearing its deadline, but a key team member is falling behind. Aabha knows that this colleague is dealing with personal issues, and while she empathises with their struggles, the delays are putting the project at risk. She feels torn, wanting to support her colleague's well-being while recognising the importance of accountability for the team's success.

Aabha decides to address the issue directly yet sensitively. She speaks with her teammate privately and begins the conversation with empathy, saying, *"I know you're juggling a lot right now, and I understand it's tough."* Then, she gently but clearly states her expectations: *"However, the quality of your work is impacting the team, and we need to keep things on track."* Finally, she proposes a collaborative solution: *"Can we work together to adjust your workload so you can meet these expectations?"*

This example illustrates that assertiveness is not about imposing one's agenda or diminishing others. As Shakti Gawain's quote suggests, true assertiveness embodies authenticity and confidence while creating space for others to do the same. It involves the delicate balance of expressing our needs and boundaries while respecting those of others.

Assertiveness with compassion transforms interactions, allowing us to communicate openly without resorting to aggression or passivity. This chapter delves into how we can cultivate this balance, drawing from emotional intelligence, respect, and mindfulness principles to navigate complex conversations.

Defining Assertiveness

Assertiveness is the ability to express one's needs, opinions, and boundaries clearly, confidently, and respectfully. At its core, assertiveness strikes a balance between advocating for oneself and showing consideration for the perspectives and feelings of others. It reflects inner confidence and a strong sense of self-worth and enables individuals to communicate openly and honestly while fostering mutual respect. This alignment of self-respect with respect for others underscores the idea that assertiveness is not merely a behaviour but a fundamental way of being.

In his book When I Say No, I Feel Guilty, psychologist Manuel J. Smith introduced the concept of assertiveness as a skill that helps individuals protect their personal boundaries without infringing on others. He argued that assertiveness allows people to express their needs and emotions effectively, reducing the stress and resentment often associated with unspoken frustrations. Smith's *Assertiveness Rights*, such as the right to say no without feeling guilty and express feelings and opinions, serve as a foundation for understanding and cultivating assertiveness.

Daniel Goleman's Emotional Intelligence also emphasises the connection between assertiveness and emotional intelligence. He identifies assertiveness as a critical skill within the social competencies of emotional intelligence, highlighting its role in fostering healthy interpersonal dynamics and effective communication. By understanding assertiveness as a skill rooted in self-awareness, respect, and emotional intelligence, individuals can navigate interactions confidently while building stronger and more meaningful relationships.

Defining Compassion

Compassion is the ability to empathise with and show genuine care for another person's feelings, experiences, and challenges. It is grounded in kindness, active listening, and a deep understanding of the shared human condition. Unlike mere sympathy, which may involve feeling for someone from a distance, compassion compels us to engage with others' struggles and extend support meaningfully.

At its essence, compassion is about creating space for the emotions and perspectives of others while maintaining a balance with our own needs. It is not about self-sacrifice or ignoring personal boundaries but about recognising and respecting another person's perspective without losing sight of your own. Compassionate communication is rooted in a mutual exchange of understanding and respect, fostering a sense of connection and trust.

Kristin Neff, a pioneer in self-compassion and author of *Self-Compassion: The Proven Power of Being Kind to Yourself*, emphasises that compassion includes self-directed and other-focused care. She argues that compassion is a skill that enhances relationships and strengthens resilience, enabling individuals to navigate challenging interactions with empathy and poise.

Research from the *Journal of Positive Psychology* highlights that compassionate communication contributes significantly to relationship satisfaction, trust, and emotional well-being. This is particularly evident in professional settings, where leaders who practice compassionate communication are shown to foster higher engagement, collaboration, and morale among team members.

Compassionate interactions involve active listening, where we truly hear and validate the other person's experiences. For example, instead of jumping to advice when a friend shares their struggles, compassion prompts us to say, "That sounds tough. I'm here for you." This simple acknowledgment can deepen connections and create a sense of safety in the relationship.

By integrating compassion into communication, we build more meaningful and respectful relationships and create environments where empathy and assertiveness can thrive harmoniously.

Bringing Assertiveness and Compassion Together

When assertiveness and compassion are combined, they create a harmonious communication style that honours both your needs and the needs of others. This balanced approach fosters respect, understanding, and collaboration, even in difficult conversations. Assertive, compassionate communication is compelling in challenging situations, where both clarity and empathy are crucial to resolving conflicts or setting boundaries without damaging relationships.

This approach involves confidently expressing your needs and boundaries while being attentive to the other person's emotions and perspectives. By blending assertiveness and compassion, you can navigate conversations with authenticity and mutual respect, turning potential conflicts into opportunities for deeper connection.

Declining a Friend's Request

Imagine a friend asks you to help them move this weekend, but you've already made plans to recharge after a hectic week. Simply declining without explanation might be dismissive, while agreeing reluctantly could lead to resentment. Here's how assertive, compassionate communication could play out:

- *Compassionate Acknowledgment:* Begin by recognising their need. For example, "I know moving can be overwhelming, and I can see why you'd want some extra hands to make it easier."

- *Assertive Boundary Setting:* Clearly express your limitations. "Unfortunately, I've had an exhausting week and need this weekend to rest."

- *Collaborative Offer:* If possible, offer an alternative or show support differently. "I'd love to help you unpack next week or lend you some boxes if needed."

This approach respects your well-being while showing care and understanding for your friend's situation. The result is a dialogue that maintains the relationship's trust and mutual respect.

Feedback at Work

Now consider a professional setting where you must give constructive feedback to a colleague whose work quality has declined. Assertiveness allows you to address the issue directly, while compassion ensures the conversation is supportive rather than aggressive.

- *Compassionate Acknowledgment:* Start by recognising their efforts. "I know you've been juggling multiple projects, and I appreciate your hard work."

- *Assertive Clarity:* Highlight the specific concern. "I noticed that the recent report had some inconsistencies that might affect the project timeline."

- *Collaborative Support:* Offer to work together to resolve the issue. "Can we go through it together and make adjustments? I'm happy to help where I can."

By combining assertiveness and compassion, this conversation encourages improvement without demotivating the colleague, fostering a more productive and positive work environment.

In essence, the synergy of assertiveness and compassion ensures that both parties feel heard, valued, and respected. It's not about compromising your needs or overshadowing others but finding a middle ground where open dialogue can lead to mutual understanding and stronger relationships.

Assertive, Compassionate Communication vs. Passive and Aggressive Styles

Assertive, compassionate communication is a balanced approach that combines confidence and empathy, distinguishing it from the extremes of passive and aggressive communication. Here's a comparison of these styles to highlight the value of assertiveness with compassion:

Passive Communication

Passive communication occurs when individuals avoid expressing their needs or opinions, often prioritising others' comfort over their own. While rooted in compassion, this approach lacks assertiveness, leading to unmet needs, unspoken resentment, or feeling overlooked.

- **Characteristics:** Avoids conflict, hesitates to speak up, and prioritises others' needs at their own expense.

  Example: A team member agrees to take on additional responsibilities despite feeling overwhelmed, fearing that declining might create tension. Over time, this can lead to burnout and frustration.

Aggressive Communication

Aggressive communication asserts one's needs or opinions forcefully, often disregarding the feelings or perspectives of others. This approach lacks compassion, prioritising personal goals without considering the relational impact.

- **Characteristics:** Forceful, controlling, and often dismissive of others' feelings.

  Example: A manager demands an urgent report completion without acknowledging the team's current workload or challenges, creating a sense of pressure and resentment within the team.

Assertive, Compassionate Communication

Assertive, compassionate communication combines the confidence of assertiveness with the care and understanding of compassion. This approach fosters mutual respect, clarity, and collaboration, ensuring that all parties feel valued and heard.

- **Characteristics:** Balances confidence and kindness, communicates needs clearly while respecting others' feelings, and seeks collaborative solutions.

  Example: A manager addresses the need for a new project deadline by acknowledging the team's workload:

  "I know you're all juggling multiple priorities right now, and I truly appreciate your hard work. We need to discuss the timeline for this new project, but let's explore how we can manage it together to avoid adding unnecessary stress."

  This approach builds trust and maintains productivity by respecting the team's efforts while addressing the need for progress.

Key Differences

Style	Focus	Outcome
Passive	Prioritises others at personal expense	Needs often go unmet, leading to frustration or resentment.
Aggressive	Prioritises self at others' expense	It creates conflict, damages relationships, and diminishes trust.
Assertive - Compassionate	Balances self and others' needs	It builds respect, fosters collaboration, and strengthens relationships.

By understanding these differences, we can see how assertive, compassionate communication fosters a collaborative environment where all voices are heard, and needs are met without compromising respect or empathy. It is the cornerstone of meaningful and effective interactions in both personal and professional settings.

Why Assertiveness with Compassion Matters

Combining assertiveness with compassion creates positive, productive interactions that strengthen relationships and promote emotional well-being. This balanced approach fosters trust and respect by valuing our needs and others' perspectives, addressing issues early to prevent conflict, and maintaining a collaborative tone during challenges. Compassionate assertiveness nurtures authenticity and deeper connections by reducing stress and empowering us to express ourselves confidently without guilt, making it a cornerstone for thriving personal and professional relationships.

Building Assertive, Compassionate Communication Skills

Mastering assertive, compassionate communication involves combining practical strategies with an awareness of Non-verbal cues to foster meaningful connections in personal and professional settings.

- *Use "I" Statements:* Express feelings without blame to maintain clarity and focus on your experience.

  "I feel overwhelmed when given multiple tasks at once. Can we prioritise them together?"

- *Set Boundaries with Kindness:* Respectfully communicating boundaries prevents misunderstandings and shows care for yourself and the relationship.

  "I'd love to help, but I must focus on my current tasks first. Can we revisit this later?"

- *Express Empathy:* Acknowledge others' perspectives while maintaining your own needs.

  "I understand this project is important to you, and I also have commitments to balance."

- *Practise Active Listening:* Attentive listening demonstrates respect and encourages collaborative problem-solving.

  "I hear that you're feeling stressed about the deadline. Can weexplore solutions together?"

- *Handle Difficult Conversations with Honesty and Care:* Approach challenging discussions calmly, balancing clarity and openness.

  "I'd like to discuss something on my mind. I value our relationship and want to find a way forward together."

The Role of Body Language in Assertive Communication

Non-verbal cues reinforce assertiveness with respect and compassion:

- *Eye Contact:* Steady eye contact conveys sincerity and engagement.
- *Open Posture:* A relaxed stance signals approachability.
- *Calm, Steady Tone:* A balanced tone keeps conversations constructive.
- *Mindful Gestures:* Open-handed gestures reflect honesty and empathy.

Applying Assertive, Compassionate Communication in Real Life

- *Personal Relationships:* Foster open communication and trust by setting boundaries with empathy.

  Example: Emma tells her partner, "I cherish our time together, and also need alone time to recharge," strengthening their bond.

- *Workplace Dynamics:* Promote inclusivity and teamwork while voicing your needs effectively.

  Example: Mark, feeling overlooked in meetings, suggests a round-robin format to ensure everyone's input is heard.

- *Self-Advocacy and Personal Boundaries:* Assertiveness paired with compassion strengthens self-respect while fostering mutual understanding.

  Example: Maria, a freelancer, sets boundaries with a client, saying, "To deliver high-quality work, I'll be available during business hours and will prioritise urgent requests within that timeframe." Her client appreciates her clarity and adjusts expectations.

By integrating assertiveness with compassion and reinforcing it with respectful body language, we can navigate complex interactions with confidence, empathy, and balance.

Summary

The chapter "Assertiveness with Compassion" delved into combining assertiveness with empathy to foster meaningful, productive interactions. It highlighted that assertiveness was not about being forceful or aggressive but about confidently expressing one's needs while respecting others. Compassion added depth by valuing the perspectives and emotions of others, creating a balanced communication approach.

The chapter explained how assertiveness and compassion allowed individuals to navigate challenging conversations, set boundaries with kindness, and maintain relationships based on trust and mutual respect. Practical strategies, such as using "I" statements, active listening, and empathy, were explored alongside the importance of Non-verbal cues like eye contact, tone, and body language. Real-life examples demonstrated how assertive, compassionate communication could enhance personal relationships, workplace dynamics, and self-advocacy. By merging these qualities, individuals could build trust, prevent conflicts, and communicate effectively in a manner that strengthened connections and emotional well-being.

Key Takeaways

- **Balance Assertiveness with Compassion:** Assertive, compassionate communication respects both personal needs and the emotions of others, creating meaningful connections.

- **Use "I" Statements for Clarity:** Expressing feelings with "I" statements prevents blame and fosters understanding.

- **Set Boundaries with Empathy:** Communicating boundaries respectfully strengthens relationships while protecting one's well-being.

- **Active Listening Enhances Trust:** Demonstrating attentiveness and empathy during conversations makes others feel valued and heard.

- **Non-verbal Cues Are Crucial:** Eye contact, tone, and posture reinforce assertiveness and compassion in communication.

- **Build Confidence and Collaboration:** Assertive, compassionate communication prevents misunderstandings, encourages inclusivity, and fosters trust.

Reflection Activities

1. **Evaluate Your Communication Style:** Reflect on a recent conversation. Did you balance assertiveness with compassion? How did your tone and body language affect the interaction?

2. **Set a Kind Boundary:** Identify a situation where you need to set a boundary. Plan how to communicate it assertively while acknowledging the other person's perspective.

3. **Observe Non-verbal Cues:** During your next interaction, pay attention to your eye contact, posture, and tone. How do these elements influence the clarity and reception of your message?

Self-Assessment Checklist

Rate yourself from 0 (Rarely) to 5 (Consistently)

1. I express my needs clearly using "I" statements, ensuring I communicate without assigning blame. ___ / 5

2. I set personal boundaries respectfully and empathetically, balancing clarity with understanding. ___ / 5

3. I practise active listening, demonstrating genuine empathy and attentiveness during conversations. ___ / 5

4. I communicate assertively while maintaining compassion, ensuring confidence is balanced with care. ___ / 5

5. I remain calm and thoughtful during challenging conversations, responding with respect and understanding. ___ / 5

Chapter 14

THE POWER OF HUMOUR: CONNECTING WITH WIT AND WARMTH

"Humour is mankind's greatest blessing."

—*Mark Twain.*

Humour is one of humanity's most universal and profound traits. From the earliest moments of human civilization, laughter has been a bridge connecting individuals, easing tensions and brightening even the darkest days. As Mark Twain so eloquently observed, humour is not merely entertainment; it is a gift, a blessing that unites us in shared joy and understanding.

The Role of Humour in Human Life

In every culture, humour transcends language, age, and social barriers. Archaeologists have unearthed ancient texts and artefacts like early Roman satire and Egyptian carvings suggesting that our ancestors valued laughter as a crucial part of life. Even in prehistoric times, tribes likely bonded around the fire with stories and humour, reinforcing social bonds and reducing stress after a day of survival.

Humour taps into our shared humanity, making us feel connected and seen. Whether it's a light-hearted jest among friends or a moment of levity in a serious conversation, humour allows us to experience collective relief, hope, and joy. It reminds us that we are not alone in our struggles or triumphs.

Why Humour Matters Today

In today's fast-paced, high-stress world, humour has become more vital than ever. As we navigate the demands of technology, professional pressures, and societal complexities, a moment of laughter can be an antidote to tension and burnout. Studies published in the *Journal of Personality and Social Psychology* reveal that shared laughter strengthens relationships and boosts team trust and collaboration.

In professional settings, humour is a subtle yet powerful tool. A manager facing tight deadlines can use a well-placed joke to lighten the mood and refocus the team. For instance, imagine a project leader walking into a tense room and quipping, "I know it feels like we're building the pyramids with toothpicks, but we'll get there!" This moment of levity shifts the energy, helping the team feel understood and motivated without diminishing the seriousness of the task.

Similarly, in personal relationships, humour serves as a balm. It diffuses conflicts, strengthens intimacy, and reminds us to take life's challenges less seriously. Consider how a simple, playful joke between partners during a disagreement can soften emotions and pave the way for resolution.

Humour: A Gift and a Skill

Humour isn't just an innate trait; it's a skill that can be cultivated. In a world filled with information overload, humour makes messages memorable, relatable, and impactful. It helps speakers captivate audiences, leaders inspire teams, and individuals navigate everyday challenges with resilience and optimism.

Mark Twain's words remind us that humour is a blessing; a uniquely human gift that enhances our lives in countless ways. By embracing humour in communication, we unlock a tool that connects us and elevates the quality of our interactions, allowing us to face life's complexities with grace and wit.

The Psychology of Humour

Why do we laugh? Why does humour make us feel lighter, more connected, and more at ease? The answers lie in the intricate interplay between our brains, emotions, and social instincts. Humour is not just a reaction; it's a complex psychological and physiological response that plays a fundamental role in human connection and well-being.

The Brain on Humour

When we encounter something funny, our brain undergoes a unique process involving the activation of multiple areas:

- **The Prefrontal Cortex:** Processes the incongruity or unexpected twist that makes a joke funny.

- **The Limbic System:** Triggers emotions like joy and surprise, reinforcing the pleasure of laughter.

- **The Motor Cortex: It** Controls the physical act of laughing, making it an embodied experience.

Research from *Nature Reviews Neuroscience* highlights that humour activates reward pathways in the brain, releasing dopamine - the "feel-good" neurotransmitter. This chemical boost makes us happy and enhances our memory and creativity, which is why humour makes ideas stick.

Emotional Benefits of Humour

1. **Stress Reduction:** Laughter lowers cortisol levels (the stress hormone) and increases endorphins, leading to relaxation and

improved mood. This is why a good laugh feels like a weight lifted off your shoulders.

2. **Enhanced Resilience:** Humour helps reframe challenges, turning setbacks into opportunities for optimism. People who can laugh at adversity often cope better with life's difficulties.

3. **Improved Social Bonding:** Shared laughter fosters a sense of closeness and trust. It creates a shared emotional experience, making individuals feel more connected and understood.

Why We Respond to Humour: **Humour resonates because it plays with expectations. At its core, humour often involves an unexpected twist, a paradox that surprises and delights us.**

For example

- **Joke Setup:** "Why don't skeletons fight each other?"
- **Punch line:** "Because they don't have the guts."

This classic wordplay subverts our expectations, engaging both our logic and emotions. This playful mismatch makes humour not only enjoyable but also memorable.

The Social Role of Humour: Humour is a social glue, helping people navigate complex dynamics and establish rapport. Whether it's breaking the ice with a stranger or easing tensions in a heated discussion, humour creates an atmosphere of goodwill and openness. A leader addressing layoffs during a difficult company meeting opens with: "I'll be brief today, just like our free coffee supply!" This self-aware, light-hearted comment acknowledges the tension without dismissing it, immediately putting the audience at ease and showing empathy.

Humour's Evolutionary Role: From an evolutionary perspective, humour likely developed as a survival tool. Anthropologists suggest that shared laughter helped early humans strengthen group bonds and defuse conflicts. It signalled safety, collaboration, and trust within social groups, essential for survival.

Humour is more than entertainment. It's a bridge to profound human connection, a tool for emotional resilience, and a catalyst for creativity and collaboration. By understanding the psychology of humour, we can harness its power in our personal and professional lives, using it to inspire, connect, and uplift.

The Practical Benefits of Humour in Communication

Humour isn't just an accessory to communication; it's a strategic tool that enhances understanding, builds relationships, and fosters a positive atmosphere. By incorporating humour thoughtfully, we can navigate complex situations, strengthen connections, and create memorable interactions.

Breaking down Barriers

Humour can dissolve tension in difficult situations, creating a neutral ground for open dialogue. It acts as a pressure valve, releasing pent-up emotions and helping people feel at ease.

In a negotiation, a client expresses concerns about costs. The negotiator responds, "Well, I've heard that free advice is worth exactly what you pay!" The light humour reduces tension, encouraging collaboration rather than conflict.

In *Humour, Seriously: Why Humour Is a Superpower at Work and in Life* by Jennifer Aaker and Naomi Bagdonas, the authors highlight that leaders who use humour effectively are perceived as 27% more motivating and admired. They emphasize that humour fosters trust and builds team cohesion.

Engaging and Retaining Attention

Humour makes messages more engaging and memorable. Speakers can use anecdotes, wordplay, or light-hearted commentary to capture their audience's attention and ensure their ideas stick.

A teacher introducing a complex topic begins with, "Statistics are like bikinis; they reveal what's interesting but hide what's crucial." This humorous analogy piques curiosity, making the subject more approachable.

Strengthening Relationships

Shared laughter creates emotional bonds. It builds rapport, deepens trust, and makes interactions more enjoyable. Humour humanizes people, fostering a sense of approachability and warmth.

A manager jokes with their team during a stressful project: "We're running on coffee and chaos, but at least we're running!" This moment of levity boosts morale and strengthens camaraderie.

Enhancing Creativity and Problem-Solving

Humour encourages outside-the-box thinking by stimulating creativity. It allows people to explore unconventional ideas without fear of judgment, fostering innovation.

During a brainstorming session, someone proposes a humorous but outlandish idea. The team laughs but then realizes that a variation of the idea could work. The playful atmosphere leads to a breakthrough solution.

Building Persuasion and Influence

Humour disarms scepticism and makes arguments more persuasive. It shows confidence and emotional intelligence, enhancing credibility.

A marketer pitching an eco-friendly product begins with, "Our product is so green, it practically photosynthesizes!" The humour captures the audience's interest and reinforces the eco-friendly message.

As Jennifer Aaker and Naomi Bagdonas explain in their book, humour doesn't just lighten the mood; it's a catalyst for connection, creativity, and persuasion. By weaving humour into our communication, we can foster trust, captivate attention, and transform mundane exchanges into memorable moments.

Types of Humour in Communication

Humour takes many forms, each with its charm and purpose. By effectively understanding and using these types, we can adapt to different contexts and audiences, enhancing connection and impact.

1. **Light-Hearted Humour:** This humour is subtle and casual, perfect for easing everyday conversations. It creates a warm, approachable atmosphere, making interactions more enjoyable and less formal.

   Example: During a team introduction, someone says, "Hi, I'm Alex, and my superpower is remembering names... for about five minutes." This light-hearted comment breaks the ice and fosters camaraderie.

   Purpose: To build rapport and make initial connections comfortable.

2. **Situational Humour:** Situational humour involves finding wit at the moment, turning everyday occurrences into opportunities for laughter. It shows adaptability and quick thinking, often diffusing tension or making interactions memorable.

Example: A speaker's microphone cuts out during a presentation, and they quip, "Looks like even the mike wants me to keep it short!" The audience laughs, and the moment becomes a shared experience rather than an interruption.

Purpose: To address unexpected moments with charm and confidence.

3. **Self-Deprecating Humour:** Laughing at oneself can be a powerful way to appear relatable and approachable. Self-deprecating humour, when used appropriately, shows humility and confidence, allowing others to see the lighter side of your personality.

   Example: A manager presenting a new idea says, "I hope this makes sense because it sounded great in my head at 2 AM!" The humour makes the leader more relatable, easing any pressure or judgment from the team.

   Purpose: To diffuse tension and establish a sense of equality, especially in hierarchical settings.

4. **Observational Humour:** This type of humour involves making witty remarks about universally relatable situations. It resonates with people by highlighting the quirks of daily life.

   Example: In a meeting about work-life balance, someone jokes, "My work-life balance is like my Wi-Fi; it's strong for a minute, then completely disappears!" The humour creates a shared understanding of a common challenge.

   Purpose: To create a connection by acknowledging shared experiences.

5. **Clever Wordplay or Puns:** Playing with words or meanings adds a creative twist to communication. It's light and fun but should be used sparingly to avoid seeming forced.

Example: At a bakery's team meeting, someone suggests, "Let's roll with the dough and rise to the occasion!" The pun brings humour while staying relevant to the context.

Purpose: To add a playful element to conversations, keeping the tone light-hearted and engaging.

Humour across Cultures: Navigating Diversity

Humour is not a one-size-fits-all approach. Cultural diversity plays a significant role in how humour is perceived, appreciated, and interpreted. What may be light-hearted and relatable in one culture could be misunderstood or even offensive in another. For example, self-deprecating humour, typical in Western cultures, might not resonate in collectivist societies where group harmony is prioritized over individual expression.

When navigating culturally diverse settings, it's essential to consider:

- **Audience Sensitivity:** Understand your audience's cultural background and preferences. Avoid humour that may touch on cultural stereotypes or sensitive topics.

- **Universal Themes:** Stick to universally relatable topics, such as everyday mishaps or shared human experiences, which transcend cultural barriers.

- **Observation and Adaptability:** Pay attention to audience reactions to refine your approach. If humour doesn't land well, quickly pivot to a neutral tone.

Example: During an international conference, a speaker used a humorous analogy about long airport queues, a universally relatable scenario. This subtle, culturally neutral humour drew laughter from a global audience, creating connection without alienating anyone.

By embracing cultural diversity in humour, you avoid pitfalls and create meaningful bridges that foster mutual respect and understanding.

Gauging Appropriateness in Sensitive Situations

Humour's power lies in its ability to diffuse tension, but misjudging its appropriateness in sensitive or high-stakes situations can have the opposite effect. To gauge whether humour is suitable:

- **Read the Room:** Observe body language, tone, and emotional cues to assess whether the audience is open to fun. A tense atmosphere might require empathy before introducing humour.

- **Context Matters:** Consider the gravity of the situation. In moments of grief, conflict, or formal discussions, humour should be used sparingly and only if it can genuinely uplift rather than detract from the moment.

- **Test with Subtlety:** Begin with a light comment or gentle humour to gauge the audience's receptiveness. If it resonates, you can proceed with confidence. If it falls flat, recalibrate your approach.

- **Ask Yourself:** "Will this humour add value or distract from the message?" A moment of self-reflection can prevent missteps.

By being mindful and adaptable, you can ensure that humour enhances rather than detracts from your message, even in delicate scenarios.

The Role of Humour in Leadership

Humour is a powerful yet underutilized tool in leadership. It can inspire, build trust, and unite teams. A leader's use of humour fosters an atmosphere of approachability, encouraging open dialogue and collaboration. It helps to humanize authority, making leaders relatable while boosting morale and reducing stress in high-pressure environments. Humour can also make complex or difficult messages more palatable, allowing leaders to communicate authentically and warmly, even when addressing serious issues.

Barack Obama exemplified the effective use of humour in leadership. Known for his wit, he often used self-deprecating jokes and light-hearted quips to disarm critics and connect with diverse audiences. For instance, during the White House Correspondents' Dinner, he humorously remarked about his graying hair: "I look in the mirror and I have to admit, I'm not the strapping young Muslim socialist that I used to be." While playful, the comment diffused criticism and stereotypes with confidence and charm.

Beyond fun, Obama's humour was purposeful. In profound moments, he used it to put audiences at ease and draw attention to important issues without overwhelming or alienating them. For example, when addressing healthcare reform, he quipped, "Let me just be clear if you like your doctor, you can keep your doctor. Unless, of course, your doctor is a goat." This clever remark lightened a complex discussion, making his message accessible while maintaining focus on the subject.

Leaders who integrate humour effectively can inspire their teams, transform tense situations into opportunities for connection, and foster an environment where people feel motivated and valued. When used wisely, humour becomes a tool for entertainment and impactful leadership.

Practical Tips for Using Humour Effectively

- *Know your audience:* Tailor your humour to the sensitivities and preferences of your audience, keeping in mind cultural, professional, and individual boundaries.

- *Start small:* Begin with gentle wit, such as a playful comment or light joke, to gauge the audience's comfort level.

- *Combine with storytelling:* Humorous anecdotes can create memorable impressions, making your message relatable and engaging.

- *Use timing wisely:* Deliver humour appropriately to ensure it enhances your message, rather than distracts from it.

- *Stay authentic:* Use humour that reflects your personality to maintain genuineness and connection.

Common Mistakes and How to Avoid Them

- *Overusing humour:* Too much humour can dilute your message or make you appear unprofessional. Balance is key.

  Avoidance Tip: Use humour sparingly to highlight key points or lighten the mood. Ensure it supports your communication goals.

- *Inappropriate jokes:* Jokes that disrespect boundaries or contexts can alienate your audience.

  Avoidance Tip: Be mindful of cultural, professional, and individual sensitivities to keep humour respectful and inclusive.

- *Misreading the audience:* Humour can fall flat if the timing or tone isn't right.

  Avoidance Tip: Pay attention to the audience's reactions and energy, and be ready to pivot if humour isn't resonating.

How Humour Shapes Connections

Humour has a unique way of breaking down barriers and creating bonds, making it one of the most powerful tools in human interaction. When used thoughtfully, it can transform tense moments into opportunities for understanding, turning strangers into friends and colleagues into collaborators. Humour fosters a sense of shared experience, reminding us of our shared humanity, even in professional or high-stakes situations.

For instance, a teacher might share a light-hearted anecdote about their learning struggles to connect with students feeling overwhelmed. Similarly, in a business setting, a leader could use humour to defuse tension during a challenging meeting, creating a more collaborative atmosphere. Research in psychology shows that laughter triggers the release of endorphins, often called "feel-good" hormones, which build trust and strengthen social bonds.

Whether it's a subtle quip that lightens the mood or a self-deprecating joke that makes you more relatable, humour shapes connections by showing vulnerability, building rapport, and leaving a lasting impression. It's not about being a comedian; it's about creating moments of joy and authenticity that deepen relationships and foster a sense of belonging.

The Risks of Overusing or Misapplying Humour

While humour is a powerful tool for connection, its overuse or misapplication can undermine its effectiveness, particularly in high-stakes or formal settings. Excessive humour harms the message, making the speaker appear unprofessional or frivolous. Misjudged jokes, especially in culturally diverse or sensitive environments, can unintentionally offend or alienate the audience, damaging trust and credibility.

For example, a leader addressing a critical business setback might lose their team's confidence if they rely too heavily on jokes, creating the impression that they are not taking the situation seriously. Similarly, humour touching personal, political, or cultural sensitivities can backfire, resulting in awkwardness or disengagement.

The key lies in balance and appropriateness. Humour should enhance, not overshadow, the core message. In formal settings, it's best to use light, context-appropriate humour sparingly, ensuring it complements the tone and purpose of the communication. By being mindful of the audience, timing, and context, you can use humour to lighten the mood without focusing on the moment's seriousness.

Lightening the Load with Laughter

Humour is more than a tool for entertainment, it is a bridge to connection, resilience, and understanding. It fosters authentic relationships, alleviates tension, and creates an environment of trust and collaboration. As Mark Twain aptly said, "Humour is mankind's greatest blessing." By embracing humour thoughtfully, you not only lighten the burdens of communication but also leave a lasting impact that is as joyful as it is meaningful.

So, start small, stay authentic, and let humour add warmth and wit to your interactions. Sometimes, a little laughter is all it takes to transform a moment and a relationship for the better.

Summary

Humour is not just a tool for entertainment it is a profound way to connect, communicate, and navigate life's complexities. From breaking down barriers to diffusing tension, humour enhances personal and professional interactions. This chapter explored the types of humour, its role in leadership, and practical strategies for incorporating humour effectively. Using wit with care and intention, humour fosters trust, builds rapport, and creates memorable, meaningful connections. The transformative power of humour lies in its ability to lighten the load while deepening bonds, making it an invaluable communication skill.

Key Takeaways

1. **Humour Builds Bridges**: Light-hearted humour fosters trust and camaraderie, strengthening connections in personal and professional relationships.

2. **Types of Humour Matter**: Understanding when and how to use situational, light-hearted, or self-deprecating humour ensures it resonates with your audience.

3. **Leadership with Humour**: Leaders who use humour inspire, unite teams, and build resilience, even in challenging times.

4. **Use Humour Intentionally**: Humour should complement, not detract from, your message. Knowing your audience and the context is key.

5. **Humour's Emotional Impact**: Laughter reduces stress, releases endorphins, and creates positive emotional bonds, enhancing communication.

Reflection Activity

1. Recall a time when humour helped you build a connection. What made it effective, and how did it change the interaction?

2. Think of a situation where humour disrupted communication. What went wrong, and what could you have done differently?

3. Identify a recent moment when a tense conversation could have benefitted from humour. How might you incorporate humour in a similar future scenario?

4. Journal how humour plays a role in your personal and professional life. How can you use it more effectively to create meaningful connections?

5. What is your natural humour style? Reflect on how it aligns with the types of humour discussed and how you can refine it.

Self-Assessment Checklist

Rate yourself from 0 (Rarely) to 5 (Consistently):

1. I use humour thoughtfully and appropriately to connect with others. ___ / 5

2. I tailor my humour to suit different audiences and cultural sensitivities. ___ / 5

3. I balance humour with seriousness to maintain professionalism when needed. ___ / 5

4. I use humour to diffuse tension and foster a positive atmosphere in challenging situations. ___ / 5

5. I embrace self-deprecating humour to show relatability without undermining my credibility. ___ / 5

Chapter 15

AUTHENTIC COMMUNICATION: INTEGRITY-DRIVEN LEADERSHIP

"The supreme quality for leadership is unquestionably integrity."

—Dwight D. Eisenhower.

Eisenhower's words, drawn from his extensive experience in leading both nations and armies, encapsulate the cornerstone of authentic leadership: integrity. Leadership is not merely about achieving goals or wielding influence; it is about inspiring trust and embodying values others can rely on. Harvard Business Review highlights that integrity consistently ranks among the top qualities of effective leaders, as it builds the trust necessary for collaboration, loyalty, and long-term success. Integrity gives leadership its moral compass, ensuring that actions align with values, words reflect the truth, and decisions serve the greater good. But what makes integrity the driving force behind transformative leadership?

Integrity in Action: Nelson Mandela's Story

Nelson Mandela's leadership epitomised integrity in its purest form. Growing up amidst apartheid's harsh realities, Mandela stood firm against racial injustice, even when faced with adversity. Despite 27 years of imprisonment, he emerged as a symbol of forgiveness and reconciliation.

Mandela's unwavering commitment to integrity was evident when he chose unity over vengeance. His powerful words, *"As I walked out the door toward the gate that would lead to my freedom, I knew if I didn't leave my bitterness and hatred behind, I'd still be in prison,"* reflect his ability to prioritise the greater good over personal grievances. Mandela's integrity inspired millions, fostering peace and equality in South Africa and earning him global admiration.

The Meaning of Integrity in Leadership

Integrity in leadership is the alignment between a leader's values, actions, and words. It involves consistently upholding ethical principles, being honest, and acting responsibly, even in difficult circumstances. Leaders with integrity inspire trust and foster loyalty because they prioritize what is right over what is convenient.

Research from *Forbes* suggests that leaders with high integrity foster greater employee engagement and satisfaction. A 2019 study published in the *Journal of Business Ethics* also highlighted that integrity-driven leadership leads to higher organizational trust, employee loyalty, and overall productivity.

A Transparent Leader during a Crisis

Imagine a school principal facing the challenging decision to temporarily close the institution due to unforeseen circumstances. Instead of issuing a brief, ambiguous notice, the principal organizes a virtual meeting with staff, students, and parents to explain the situation in detail. They openly discuss the reasons for the closure, the potential timeline for reopening, and how the school plans to support students' learning during the interim.

The principal also provides opportunities for attendees to voice their concerns, addressing each question with empathy and clarity. After the meeting, they followed up with a detailed email outlining the key points discussed and providing contact information for further queries. By proactively communicating and showing accountability, the principal gains the community's trust and reassures everyone that their concerns are being considered.

Understanding Integrity in Communication

Integrity in communication means being honest, consistent, and reliable in what we say and do. It involves aligning our words with our actions, providing clarity, and being transparent even when delivering complex messages. For leaders, this ensures that their teams can trust their guidance and decisions.

Studies by *Harvard Business Review* emphasize that consistency in communication builds trust. Leaders who frequently align their words with actions are perceived as more authentic and dependable. In his work on emotional intelligence, Daniel Goleman underscores that integrity in communication fosters trust and deepens relationships by ensuring that people feel heard, valued, and respected.

A CEO Navigating a Communication Breakdown

Imagine a CEO discovering that a recent policy change has caused confusion and frustration among employees due to a lack of clarity in communication. Instead of ignoring the feedback or shifting blame, the CEO immediately addresses the issue.

They hold a company-wide town hall meeting to acknowledge the oversight, stating, "I understand the rollout of this policy wasn't as clear as it should have been, and I take responsibility for that." The CEO then explains the intent behind the policy, outlines the steps to provide more detailed guidance, and invites employees to share their concerns and suggestions.

After the meeting, the CEO ensures follow-up by distributing a clear, actionable document that addresses the points raised and provides a channel for ongoing feedback. This transparent and responsive approach resolves the immediate confusion and reinforces the CEO's commitment to open, honest communication.

Integrity as a Foundation for Trust

Building trust through integrity is essential in leadership. For instance, consider Jacinda Ardern, the former Prime Minister of New Zealand. During challenging times like the Christchurch shootings and the COVID-19 pandemic, she communicated with honesty and compassion. She didn't just say what people wanted to hear; she was transparent, explaining the challenges and sharing hard truths. People trusted her because she treated them as partners, not just listeners. Her integrity built trust, bringing New Zealanders together in unity and strength.

Suppose you're managing a project, and there is a delay. Instead of hiding it, you inform your team, explaining the reasons and the plan to move forward. This transparency fosters trust, showing that you value honesty over appearances.

Leaders who communicate with integrity create a safe, respectful environment where team members feel encouraged to contribute openly. This trust nurtures a shared commitment to common goals and unites individuals toward a meaningful purpose. Recall a time when someone's honesty made you feel safe to express your ideas. How did that influence your trust in them?

Why Integrity in Communication Matters

Integrity in communication is more than choosing the right words or presenting a polished image, it's about building trust and fostering genuine connections. When leaders communicate with authenticity, consistency, and reliability, they create an environment where honesty becomes the norm and respect is a given. This atmosphere encourages open dialogue, collaboration, and meaningful interactions.

Leaders who uphold integrity in their communication set the tone for their teams, demonstrating the importance of aligning words with actions. They inspire others to follow suit by being transparent and dependable, fostering a culture where openness, accountability, and trust thrive. Integrity in communication doesn't require perfection, it calls for consistency and a commitment to staying true to principles, even in the face of adversity.

Imagine a team or organisation that consistently practices integrity in communication. Such a culture encourages employees to speak up without fear, share ideas freely, and address issues constructively. This openness enhances team dynamics and drives innovation and resilience, as everyone feels valued and understood.

Practical Strategies for Integrity-Driven Leadership

Leading with integrity isn't just about making the right decisions, it's about cultivating an environment where honesty, trust, and respect are deeply embedded. Leaders who prioritize integrity inspire confidence and collaboration within their teams. Here's how to lead with integrity effectively:

1. **Be Transparent**

   Share the bigger picture with your team, providing context for your decisions and feedback. Transparency fosters trust and helps team members see how their roles contribute to larger goals.

- *Example*: During a challenging project delay, a manager openly communicates the reasons behind the delay, acknowledges the challenges, and discusses actionable steps to overcome them, reinforcing trust within the team.

2. **Own Mistakes and Demonstrate Accountability**

Acknowledge errors and focus on solutions rather than shifting blame. This humility strengthens your credibility and encourages others to take responsibility for their actions.

- *Example*: A leader admits, "I underestimated the time needed for this task. Let's reassess our approach to meet the deadline together," showing accountability and fostering a collaborative mindset.

3. **Encourage Open Dialogue**

Create an environment where team members can confidently voice their ideas and concerns. Active listening and acknowledging diverse perspectives build a culture of respect and innovation.

- *Example*: In team meetings, a leader invites input from quieter members by saying, "I'd love to hear your perspective on this it's valuable to have all viewpoints."

4. **Align Values and Actions**

Consistently align your actions with your stated values to reinforce trust and integrity. Recognize and celebrate contributions that embody these shared principles.

- *Example*: A leader who prioritizes teamwork publicly acknowledges a team member's effort to assist a struggling colleague, reinforcing the value of collaboration.

5. **Empower Through Trust**

   Avoid micromanaging by trusting your team to take ownership of their responsibilities. This empowerment fosters growth and accountability.

   - *Illustration*: A leader assigns a challenging task to a team member, providing guidance but allowing them the autonomy to execute it. This approach builds confidence and competence.

The Impact of Integrity on Team

- *Boosts Team Morale:* Trust and respect create a safe space where team members feel valued and motivated to contribute.

- *Promotes Accountability:* Leaders who model integrity inspire others to take ownership of their actions, fostering collective responsibility.

- *Encourages Genuine Collaboration:* Respect and trust-driven environments enable open dialogue and unified efforts toward shared goals.

- *Builds a Unified, Respectful Culture:* Integrity strengthens the foundation of respect and shared values, resulting in higher team performance and morale.

Key Dimensions of Integrity-Driven Leadership

Dimension	Key Insight	Actionable Example
Ethical Leadership	Aligns decisions with core values, fostering trust and credibility.	A manager chooses transparency over hiding setbacks, openly discussing challenges and solutions with their team.

Dimension	Key Insight	Actionable Example
Integrity in Crisis Management	Integrity is tested in high-pressure scenarios and strengthens trust when upheld.	A leader prioritises safety over profit during a crisis, communicating transparently and taking accountability for decisions.
Challenges to Maintaining Integrity	Leaders face pressure to compromise values but must uphold principles.	An executive declines a lucrative deal that conflicts with company ethics, reinforcing a culture of integrity.
Measuring Integrity in Leadership	Trust, consistency, and ethical decision-making are indicators of integrity.	A survey reveals that team members feel consistently supported and respected, reflecting a leader's integrity.
Role of Emotional Intelligence	EI complements integrity, enabling empathetic and thoughtful communication.	A leader uses active listening and empathy to understand a team member's challenges, fostering a culture of respect.
Integrity Across Cultures	Cultural nuances influence how integrity is perceived and communicated.	A global leader adapts their communication style to align with local customs while maintaining honesty and authenticity.

Reflect on these dimensions of integrity in your leadership. Identify one area where you can enhance your approach, and take a specific action this week to reinforce trust and authenticity in your interactions.

Integrity as a Lifelong Leadership Commitment

Integrity is not a destination; it's a journey, an ongoing practice of aligning your values, actions, and words. Every decision you make, every conversation you have, and every challenge you face is an opportunity to lead with authenticity and purpose. Integrity is the cornerstone of trust and respect and the catalyst for meaningful change in your team, organization, and life.

Authentic leadership isn't about titles or accolades; it's about the impact you create through your unwavering commitment to doing what's right, even when it's hard. Leading with integrity inspires others to reach their potential, fostering a culture of accountability, collaboration, and growth.

Integrity-driven leadership is more than a practice; it's a legacy. Your commitment to integrity can transform your leadership and the lives of those you lead. Start today, and let integrity be the hallmark of your leadership journey.

Summary

Integrity forms the bedrock of effective leadership. Leaders who align their actions with values foster environments where teams feel safe, respected, and motivated to excel. This chapter explored the transformative power of integrity in shaping communication, decision-making, and team dynamics. Practical strategies for leading by example were discussed, emphasising the importance of consistency, accountability, and empathy in leadership. Upholding integrity isn't just about achieving goals; it's about inspiring a culture of trust, collaboration, and mutual growth, ensuring long-term success and meaningful impact.

Key Takeaways

- **Integrity Builds Trust:** Trust is the foundation of strong teams and is reinforced when leaders prioritise honesty and fairness.

- **Authenticity Inspires Influence:** Staying true to one's values fosters respect and inspires others to follow confidently.

- **Consistency and Accountability Matter:** Leaders who consistently align their words with actions set a standard of reliability and trustworthiness.

- **Challenges Reveal Character:** Upholding integrity in adversity strengthens credibility and respect.

- **Growth through Reflection:** Leading with integrity requires regular self-reflection and a commitment to personal and professional growth.

Reflection Activity

1. Reflect on a situation where maintaining integrity under pressure was difficult. How did you navigate it, and what could you have done differently?

2. Consider whether your actions consistently align with your words. What adjustments, if any, could reinforce trust in your leadership?

3. Identify one specific way to effectively model integrity in your daily interactions.

4. Recall a moment when your integrity was tested. How did your response impact your team's perception of your leadership?

5. Assess the role your integrity plays in fostering team morale. How can you enhance its positive influence?

Self-Assessment Checklist

Rate yourself from 0 (Rarely) to 5 (Consistently):

1. I consistently align my actions with my words. ___ / 5

2. I uphold honesty and transparency, even in challenging situations. ___ / 5

3. I create a safe and inclusive environment where team members feel valued and heard. ___ / 5

4. I take full accountability for my decisions and openly admit mistakes when they occur. ___ / 5

5. I actively encourage and model integrity in my team's daily interactions. ___ / 5

Chapter 16

COMMUNICATION:
THE EVOLVING PATH FOR LIFELONG GROWTH

"Communication – the human connection –
is the key to personal and career success."

—Paul J. Meyer

Growth isn't a destination; it's a journey that requires us to adapt, evolve, and refine our abilities over time. Among the many skills that fuel this journey, communication stands out as the cornerstone of both personal and professional success. It's not merely about speaking or listening; it's about creating meaningful connections, building trust, and fostering understanding in a world that's constantly changing.

Mastering communication is not a one-time achievement but a lifelong commitment to growth. It's about embracing curiosity, being open to feedback, and finding new ways to express and understand. This chapter delves into why communication remains an essential tool for lifelong growth, offering insights and strategies to help you keep this skill alive and impactful at every stage of your life.

Whether it's navigating the complexities of relationships, leading with integrity, or simply connecting authentically, communication is your bridge to deeper connections and greater achievements. Let's explore how to cultivate and evolve this skill to make a lasting impact on your journey.

Communication as a Lifelong Skill

Warren Buffett, one of the world's most celebrated investors, offers a powerful example of how communication can transform personal and professional growth. Despite his unparalleled business acumen, Buffett has repeatedly credited his success not solely to financial expertise but to his ability to communicate effectively. Early in his career, however, this was far from the case. Terrified of public speaking, Buffett's fear was so profound that it almost prevented him from achieving his aspirations.

Instead of letting this fear define him, Buffett decided to face his challenges head-on. Enrolling in a Dale Carnegie course on public speaking, he diligently worked to overcome his fear, developing clarity and confidence in how he expressed his ideas. Today, Buffett's communication skills are as renowned as his investment strategies, enabling him to inspire trust, connect with audiences, and lead with influence.

Buffett's journey demonstrates that communication is not an innate talent reserved for a select few but a skill that can be cultivated and refined with dedication. It is a continuous process, a practice that evolves as we grow. His example shows that regardless of where we start, a commitment to improving our communication skills can ripple through every aspect of life, empowering us to lead, connect, and succeed with a more significant impact.

Why It Matters

Why dedicate yourself to improving communication throughout your life? Because the impact is undeniable. Communication isn't just about exchanging words; it's the foundation of connection, trust, and understanding. In relationships, strong communication nurtures emotional bonds, fosters empathy, and helps navigate challenges, creating meaningful, lasting connections.

Professionally, it's the key to collaboration, clarity, and creativity. Great communicators inspire teamwork, foster innovation, and align people toward common goals. It's the skill that turns ideas into action and potential into achievement.

By making communication a lifelong practice, you're equipping yourself with a tool that transcends all aspects of life. It becomes the foundation for resilience, personal growth, and creating meaningful connections that truly stand the test of time.

The Evolution of Communication

Communication, much like personal and professional growth, is not static. It evolves with life's stages, challenges, and opportunities. What begins as simple expressions of needs in childhood transforms into complex dialogues that shape relationships, careers, and legacies. Each phase of life requires us to adapt our communication style, expanding our capacity to connect, influence, and inspire.

Adapting through Life's Phases

1. **Personal Relationships: From Understanding to Empathy** Early in life, communication often revolves around expressing needs and establishing connections. As relationships mature, the emphasis shifts to listening, empathy, and understanding. For example, resolving conflicts with a partner or strengthening bonds with family often demands a blend of assertiveness and compassion.

2. **Career Growth: Clarity and Collaboration** In the workplace, communication becomes a tool for collaboration and influence. Early career stages require clarity, the ability to ask the right

questions and active listening. As one progresses, leadership roles demand a shift from simply relaying information to inspiring and empowering teams. Communication here becomes a blend of transparency, vision-sharing, and emotional intelligence.

3. **Leadership Roles: Inspiring Through Connection** - At the peak of one's career, communication takes on a broader, more impactful role. Leaders must adapt their style to resonate with diverse teams, navigate crises, and foster cultures of trust and innovation. Adapting communication styles becomes essential not only for achieving goals but also for leaving a legacy.

Satya Nadella: A Modern Example of Evolved Communication

Satya Nadella, Microsoft's CEO, exemplifies the evolution of communication through adaptability and emotional intelligence. When he became CEO in 2014, Microsoft was seen as a company losing its edge. Nadella recognised that a transformation was needed in products, services, and culture.

- **Empathy as a Core Communication Tool**: Nadella's leadership style was rooted in empathy. Influenced by personal experiences, including raising a son with special needs, he understood the power of listening and connection. He championed a culture of empathy at Microsoft, encouraging open dialogue and fostering collaboration.

- **Adapting to Challenges**: Nadella communicated a bold vision for the company's future, shifting its focus to cloud computing and AI. However, he also embraced humility, openly discussing failures and encouraging teams to learn from mistakes. His transparency and willingness to adapt resonated with employees and stakeholders alike.

- **Building Bridges across Boundaries**: Nadella's ability to communicate across cultures and industries helped Microsoft rebuild trust and partnerships. His approachable and inclusive communication style transformed the company's internal dynamics and external relationships.

Today, under Nadella's leadership, Microsoft is thriving financially and recognized as a company that prioritizes innovation, inclusivity, and trust qualities made possible by his evolved approach to communication.

Lessons from Evolved Communicators

Whether nurturing relationships, climbing the career ladder, or leading organizations, communication must evolve to meet life's demands. Leaders like Satya Nadella show adaptability, empathy, and transparency, which are key to effectively navigating these changes. By reflecting on our communication styles and embracing growth, we can transform how we connect with others and the impact we leave behind.

What phase of your life requires a shift in communication? How can you adapt to meet the moment?

Building a Legacy through Communication

Mastering communication is more than a tool for personal and professional success it's the foundation for creating a lasting legacy. Through the power of words, actions, and connections, we can inspire, guide, and uplift those around us, leaving an indelible mark on the lives we touch. Whether through storytelling, mentoring, or empowering others, communication becomes the bridge that connects our values and vision with the future.

Oprah Winfrey, a global media icon, has built her legacy by using storytelling to connect with people on a deeply emotional level. From her interviews to her journey, Oprah's stories inspire resilience, self-discovery, and transformation, impacting millions of lives.

Mentoring: Guiding the Next Generation

Mentorship is another powerful way to build a legacy through communication. Mentors shape future leaders by sharing insights, experiences, and encouragement, leaving a ripple effect that extends far beyond their own lifetime. Mentorship isn't just about teaching; it's about listening, understanding, and empowering others to realize their potential.

Maya Angelou, the renowned poet and activist, mentored countless individuals, including Oprah Winfrey. Her wisdom and guidance, delivered through conversations and her literary work, empowered others to embrace their authentic selves and become voices for change.

Empowering Others: Inspiring Action

Communication that empowers endures. Leaders who give others the tools to succeed, whether through clear guidance, encouragement, or belief in their abilities, create a culture of growth and positivity. Empowering communication doesn't just solve problems; it enables others to thrive independently.

Mahatma Gandhi's ability to communicate his vision of nonviolence and self-reliance inspired a nation to rise against colonial rule. Gandhi's legacy is not only in India's independence but in the global movements for justice and peace that his words and actions continue to inspire.

The Transformative Power of Communication

Consider Fred Rogers, known to millions as "Mister Rogers." Through his gentle, sincere communication on *Mister Rogers' Neighbourhood*, he taught children (and adults) about empathy, self-worth, and kindness. His ability to connect on a human level left a legacy that continues to resonate. Fred Rogers once said, "There's no person in the whole world like you, and I like you just the way you are." These simple words, communicated with authenticity and care, have transformed countless lives, reminding us of the lasting impact of compassionate communication.

What Will Your Legacy Be?

Every conversation, every story, and every word spoken with intention contributes to the legacy you leave behind. As you navigate your journey, ask yourself:

- How can my communication inspire and empower others?

- What stories am I sharing to guide and uplift those around me?

- In what ways can I use my words to shape a better future?

By mastering communication and using it as a force for good, you create a legacy that outlasts your actions, living on in the hearts and minds of others.

Your Personal Communication Blueprint

Effective communication is not a destination but a journey of continuous growth and self-reflection. Crafting your communication blueprint empowers you to improve steadily and intentionally, adapting to the evolving needs of your relationships, career, and personal goals. This section will guide you in creating a roadmap for refining your communication skills, offering practical exercises and actionable steps to help you grow.

Step 1: Assess Your Current Strengths and Areas for Growth

Take a moment to reflect on your current communication style. Ask yourself:

- Do I listen actively or often focus on how I'll respond?
- Can I express my thoughts clearly and confidently in different settings?
- Do I adapt my tone and style based on the context and audience?

Write down three strengths in your communication style and three areas you'd like to improve. For example:

- Strength: I'm empathetic and understand others' emotions.
- Improvement: I want to become more concise and impactful when presenting ideas.

Step 2: Set Short-Term and Long-Term Goals

Establish clear, actionable goals to enhance your communication. Short-term goals keep you focused on immediate improvements, while long-term aspirations motivate you to dream big.

Short-Term Goal Examples

- Become a better listener by practicing active listening techniques during daily conversations.
- Replace filler words like "um" and "like" with pauses to maintain clarity in speech.

Long-Term Goal Examples

- Develop storytelling skills to captivate audiences in professional presentations.

- Work toward becoming an inspirational speaker who influences and empowers others.

  Write one short-term and one long-term goal for your communication journey. Attach a deadline to each, such as improving active listening within one month or delivering a public speech within a year.

Step 3: Practise Daily and Build Momentum

Consistent practice is the key to mastery. Incorporate small, intentional communication exercises into your daily routine.

Daily Practices

- Dedicate 10 minutes to journaling your thoughts to improve clarity and articulation.

- Actively listen during one conversation, paraphrasing what the other person says to confirm understanding.

- Practice speaking slowly and confidently when sharing an idea at work or home.

Exercise: Keep a daily communication log to track your progress. Note one success and one area for improvement each day.

Step 4: Learn from Role Models

Study the communication styles of individuals you admire, such as leaders, speakers, or authors. Observe how they use tone, body language, and storytelling to connect with their audience.

Choose a role model (e.g., Satya Nadella for empathetic leadership or Brené Brown for vulnerability and connection). Watch a speech or read their work, and list three techniques you'd like to incorporate into your communication style.

Step 5: Seek Feedback and Reflect

Invite constructive feedback from trusted colleagues, friends, or mentors. Honest insights help you identify blind spots and refine your approach.

Ask someone you trust, "What's one thing I do well in communication, and what's one thing I could improve?" Reflect on their feedback and adjust your strategies accordingly.

Step 6: Revisit and Revise Your Blueprint

As you grow, your goals and strategies will evolve. Reassess your communication blueprint regularly to ensure it aligns with your current aspirations.

Set a reminder every three months to review your progress. Ask yourself:

- What have I improved since my last check-in?
- What new goals can I set for the coming months?

Start Today

Your communication journey begins now. Reflect on what you've learned, identify where you want to grow, and take that first step. Whether it's practicing active listening in your next conversation, setting a goal to tell your story more confidently, or seeking feedback from a trusted mentor, every action moves you closer to becoming a masterful communicator.

Ask yourself

- What will my next step be?
- How will I use my voice to connect, inspire, and empower?

Start your journey today because the most impactful changes begin with the smallest steps.

The Endless Journey of Connection

Communication is more than a skill; it's a living, evolving expression of who we are and how we connect with the world. It's the bridge between hearts, the thread that weaves relationships, and the tool that transforms ideas into impact. This journey doesn't end with mastery; it grows with every conversation, every challenge, and every moment of understanding.

Every word you speak, every pause you take, and every emotion you share is an opportunity to create deeper connections. Communication isn't about perfection; it's about authenticity. It's about showing up as yourself, being present, and leaving each interaction better than you found it.

Remember this: The world needs your voice, not a polished, flawless version, but the real, imperfect, and powerful you. Start each day with the intention to connect, inspire, and listen because, in the endless journey of communication, every step brings us closer to understanding, compassion, and unity.

Ask yourself

- How will I connect today?
- What story will I share?
- Who will I empower with my words?

Your journey begins now, and its possibilities are as endless as the connections you create.

Summary

Communication is not just a skill but a lifelong journey of growth and connection. This chapter explored the evolving nature of communication across different life stages and the importance of building a legacy through meaningful interactions and creating a personal communication blueprint for continuous improvement. Mastering communication enables individuals to inspire, empower, and leave a lasting impact through adaptability, storytelling, mentoring, and collaboration. The journey of connection is endless, urging us to grow, connect, and inspire daily.

Key Takeaways

- **Communication is Evolving:** It adapts as life changes, whether in relationships, professional growth, or leadership roles.

- **Building a Legacy:** Mastering communication allows individuals to inspire others, share meaningful stories, and empower those around them.

- **Personal Growth:** A communication roadmap helps identify goals, refine skills, and embrace continuous improvement.

- **The Power of Authenticity:** Authentic and meaningful communication fosters trust and deepens relationships.

- **Connection is Endless:** Communication is not a destination but an ongoing journey of learning, growing, and inspiring others.

Reflection Activity

1. Reflect on when improving your communication led to a breakthrough in your personal or professional life. What did you learn from that experience?

2. Identify one communication challenge you've faced recently. How could you approach it differently next time?

3. Consider someone whose communication style you admire. What qualities make them effective? How can you incorporate these into your interactions?

4. What story from your life could you share to inspire or connect with others?

5. Write down one short-term and one long-term communication goal. What steps will you take to achieve them?

Self-Assessment Checklist

Rate each from 0 (Rarely) to 5 (Consistently):

1. I actively seek growth opportunities in communication. ___ / 5

2. I adjust my communication style based on context. ___ / 5

3. I strive for clarity and consistency in interactions. ___ / 5

4. I practise resilience and patience during challenges. ___ / 5

5. I encourage collaboration by valuing others' perspectives. ___ / 5

Part 4: Communicating for Lasting Impact, Situational Skill Building

Instructions: Reflect on the scenarios below and apply insights from Part 4, focusing on empathy, assertiveness, and self-awareness to build lasting connections.

1. *A loved one shares a problematic experience with you, and you're unsure how to respond. How could you practice compassionate listening and show empathy without judgment?*

2. *You're in a position of authority and need to set boundaries with someone who keeps asking for exceptions. How can you assert your boundaries while maintaining respect and understanding?*

3. *You're reconnecting with an old friend who seems to have changed significantly. How would you approach the conversation openly, allowing for mutual growth and understanding?*

4. *You have been asked to lead a community group, but some members are sceptical of your ideas. How could you use empathy and assertiveness to encourage open dialogue and gain their trust?*

5. *A family member often interrupts and dominates conversations. How could you respectfully express your need for conversation balance to foster a healthier dynamic?*

6. *You're working with a mentee who struggles with self-confidence. How can you use compassionate, constructive feedback to encourage them while respecting their pace of growth?*

CONCLUSION

**ELEVATING YOUR LIFE
THROUGH COMMUNICATION**

"The quality of your life is the quality of your communication."

—Tony Robbins.

As we reach the final pages of this journey, it's time to reflect on the transformative power of communication. Communication is not merely a skill but a bridge. It connects our inner world with the outer, our aspirations with our actions, and our intentions with the understanding of others. This silent force shapes relationships, steers careers, and defines the quality of our lives.

Throughout this book, we've explored the multifaceted nature of communication: its foundations, evolution, and ability to transform. Whether you approached these chapters as a professional refining leadership, a parent yearning for deeper connections, or an individual seeking personal growth, these lessons were designed to resonate across all areas of life.

The Foundations We Built

We began by peeling back the layers of communication. Beyond words lie tone, gestures, and intent. From mastering self-awareness to understanding the art of listening, this section laid the groundwork for meaningful dialogue.

- **Understanding Yourself**: Communication begins within. Recognizing your patterns, strengths, and areas for growth creates the foundation for external success.

- **Listening as an Act of Connection**: True listening is not just hearing but understanding. It is a gift that deepens relationships and fosters trust.

- **Breaking Barriers**: Addressing common communication pitfalls equipped us to navigate difficult conversations gracefully and clearly.

Transforming the Way We Connect

In exploring outward communication, we discovered how intentionality, clarity, and empathy transform our interactions.

- **Clarity in Purpose**: Expressing yourself with intention ensures your message lands as intended.

- **Empathy as a Guiding Force**: Walking in another's shoes strengthens connections, reduces conflict, and builds trust.

- **Bridging Differences**: Communication became a tool for inclusion and collaboration from cultural nuances to conflict resolution.

Adapting in a Changing World

Communication has never been more complex or vital in a digitally driven, globally connected era. This part taught us how to remain authentic amidst these challenges.

- **Digital Mindfulness**: Crafting clear, intentional messages in emails, video calls, and texts ensures connection in virtual spaces.

- **Cross-Cultural Sensitivity**: Embracing diversity enriches our perspectives, transforming communication into a force for unity.

- **The Role of Storytelling**: Narratives became a bridge to share experiences, inspire action, and make even the most complex ideas relatable.

Leaving a Legacy through Communication

The final chapters focused on the lasting impact of communication and how it shapes our legacy. Leadership, authenticity, and growth created a powerful toolkit for transformative connections.

- **Integrity as a Cornerstone**: True influence comes from alignment between words and actions. Authenticity fosters trust and respect.

- **Compassionate Assertiveness**: Balancing confidence with empathy ensures that boundaries are respected while relationships are nurtured.

- **The Power of Humour**: Wit lightens tense moments, fosters approachability, and builds bridges in even the most challenging conversations.

- **The Lifelong Journey**: Communication is an evolving skill that grows as we grow, supporting resilience, collaboration, and connection.

A Celebration of Accomplishment

By reaching this point, you haven't just read a book. You've embarked on a journey to elevate your communication, transforming how you express yourself and connect with others. You've explored emotional intelligence, non-verbal cues, storytelling, humour, and authenticity.

Final Reflection: Your Path Forward

This book isn't the end; it's a beginning. Every interaction becomes an opportunity to listen deeply, express intentionally, and connect authentically. Let communication be your compass, guiding you toward growth, understanding, and meaningful relationships.

As you close this chapter, remember that every conversation can change lives, yours and those you touch, move and inspire with your connection.

How will you use your voice? How will you create your legacy?

The next step is yours to take. Go forth, communicate, and elevate.

REAL-LIFE SCENARIOS AND SOLUTIONS FOR EFFECTIVE COMMUNICATION

Understanding theory is essential in communication, but seeing it in action is where transformation begins. This section bridges the gap between concepts and practice by presenting relatable real-life scenarios from personal and professional contexts. Whether navigating difficult conversations, enhancing team collaboration, or building stronger relationships, these examples illustrate ineffective and effective approaches, offering actionable insights for meaningful change.

Each scenario aligns with the core themes of this book, providing a practical toolkit for overcoming challenges and fostering connection. Use these scenarios as a reflective guide to identify similar patterns in your life and discover strategies to elevate your communication skills step by step.

Part 1: Foundations of Effective Communication

Personal Scenario: Listening with Empathy

Ineffective: A friend shares their struggles, and you respond, "You're overthinking this; it's not that serious." The friend feels dismissed and less likely to share in the future.

Effective: You respond with, "That sounds overwhelming. Do you want to talk more about it or take a break and figure out a plan later?" This shows empathy and validates their emotions.

Problem-Solution Framework

- **Problem**: Interrupting or dismissing someone's feelings can destroy communication and harm trust.

- **Solution**: Focus on active listening. Avoid interrupting or offering unsolicited advice. Instead, ask open-ended questions like, "How can I support you right now?"

ଝଝଝ

Professional Scenario: Seeking Feedback

Ineffective: During a project review, you present your work but don't invite feedback, assuming silence means agreement. Later, you find out team members had concerns they didn't voice.

Effective: You conclude your presentation by saying, "I'd appreciate your thoughts on this. What's working? What can we improve together?" This opens the door for constructive dialogue.

Problem-Solution Framework:

- **Problem**: Avoiding feedback can lead to misunderstandings, missed opportunities for improvement, and disengaged teams.

- **Solution**: Actively seek feedback by creating a safe space. Use specific prompts like, "What's one thing we could do differently to improve this process?"

ଝଝଝ

Personal Scenario: Responding to Non-Verbal Cues

Ineffective: At a family dinner, someone is reticent, but you don't address it, thinking, "If it's important, they'll say something." They feel ignored and withdraw further.

Effective: You notice their silence and gently ask, "You seem quieter than usual. Everything is okay? I'm here if you want to talk." This demonstrates care and attentiveness.

Problem-Solution Framework:

Problem: Ignoring non-verbal cues can create emotional distance and relationship misunderstandings.

Solution: Pay attention to body language and tone. Address changes in behaviour with curiosity and care, not pressure.

❦❦❦

Professional Scenario: Encouraging Inclusivity in Meetings

Ineffective: A team member raises a point during a meeting, but you move to the next topic without acknowledging it. They feel undervalued and stop contributing.

Effective: You pause to say, "That's an interesting perspective. Can you expand on that for the group?" This makes them feel seen and encourages further input.

Problem-Solution Framework:

- **Problem:** Overlooking contributions discourages engagement and limits team creativity.

- **Solution:** Practice inclusive facilitation by acknowledging and inviting perspectives. Use phrases like "Let's explore that idea further" to encourage participation.

ৰৰৰ

Personal Scenario: Navigating Emotional Conversations

Ineffective: A loved one expresses frustration, and you respond defensively: "Why are you blaming me? I didn't do anything wrong." This escalates the conflict.

Effective: You say, "I hear you're upset, and I want to understand what's bothering you. Let's talk it through." This defuses tension and opens the door for resolution.

Problem-Solution Framework:

- **Problem:** Defensive responses can escalate emotional conversations, making it harder to resolve issues.

- **Solution:** Use reflective listening to acknowledge emotions. Respond calmly and ask clarifying questions to find common ground.

ৰৰৰ

Professional Scenario: Delivering Feedback with Care

Ineffective: You tell a colleague, "Your work needs improvement," without offering specific examples or solutions. They feel criticized and demotivated.

Effective: You say, "I appreciate your effort on this project. Here's one area we can strengthen. Let's brainstorm how to tackle it together." This balances constructive feedback with support.

Problem-Solution Framework:

- **Problem:** Generalized or negative feedback can damage morale and lead to defensiveness.

- **Solution:** Offer specific, actionable feedback paired with encouragement. Frame it as a collaborative effort, not a critique.

ଔଔଔ

Part 2: Transforming How You Communicate

Personal Scenario: Resolving Conflict

Ineffective: A close friend misses a commitment, and you say, "You always let me down. Why should I even bother anymore?" The accusatory tone escalates the tension.

Effective: You say, "I was counting on you, and I felt disappointed when you couldn't make it. Can we talk about what happened and how we can avoid this in the future?" This approach addresses the issue while preserving the relationship.

Problem-Solution Framework:

- **Problem:** Accusatory language during conflicts alienates others and prevents resolution.

- **Solution:** Use "I" statements to express feelings and needs without blaming. Frame the conversation as a shared effort to improve.

ଔଔଔ

Professional Scenario: Handling Difficult Conversations

Ineffective: You deliver feedback to a team member by saying, "You didn't meet expectations on this project," without specifics. They feel criticized and uncertain about how to improve.

Effective: You say, "I noticed some challenges with meeting the deadlines on this project. Let's discuss what factors might have contributed and how we can address them moving forward." This turns a critique into a constructive dialogue.

Problem-Solution Framework:

- **Problem:** Vague or negative feedback can demoralize and create defensiveness.

- **Solution:** Focus on specific observations and invite collaboration for improvement. Approach the conversation with curiosity, not judgment.

☙☙☙

Personal Scenario: Building Emotional Connections

Ineffective: A family member shares a personal struggle, and you respond, "I've been through worse; you'll be fine." This dismisses their feelings.

Effective: You say, "That sounds tough. I'm here for you. How can I help?" This response validates their emotions and strengthens their bond.

Problem-Solution Framework:

- **Problem:** Dismissing emotions shut down opportunities for deeper connections.

- **Solution:** Show empathy by acknowledging their feelings and offering support. Ask open-ended questions to invite further sharing.

&&&

Professional Scenario: Aligning Communication with Goals

Ineffective: In a team meeting, you focus entirely on the problems without discussing solutions. The team leaves feeling demotivated and unclear about the next steps.

Effective: You outline challenges and follow up with actionable solutions, saying, "Here are the obstacles we're facing, but I think we can overcome them by focusing on [specific actions]. What ideas do you have to move forward?" This inspires engagement and collaboration.

Problem-Solution Framework:

- **Problem:** Dwelling on problems without solutions creates negativity and confusion.
- **Solution:** Balance discussions by addressing challenges with actionable steps. Encourage team input to foster ownership.

&&&

Personal Scenario: Navigating Sensitive Topics

Ineffective: When discussing a sensitive topic with a partner, you say, "You never understand what I'm saying," which triggers defensiveness and escalates the conflict.

Effective: You say, "I feel like we're not on the same page right now. Can we take a moment to understand each other better?" This shifts the focus to mutual understanding.

Problem-Solution Framework:

- **Problem:** Blaming language creates resistance and deepens misunderstandings.

- **Solution:** Use neutral, inclusive language to keep the conversation focused on finding solutions.

🙠🙠🙠

Professional Scenario: Encouraging Team Collaboration

Ineffective: You dominate team discussions, making decisions unilaterally. Team members feel excluded and stop contributing.

Effective: You invite participation by saying, "I'd love to hear your thoughts; what approach do you think would work best for this project?" This empowers the team and fosters collaboration.

Problem-Solution Framework:

- **Problem:** A lack of inclusivity stifles creativity and team morale.

- **Solution:** Actively invite input and encourage diverse perspectives. Acknowledge contributions to build a sense of value and ownership.

🙠🙠🙠

Part 3: Communication in the Modern World

Personal Scenario: Misinterpreting Digital Communication

Ineffective: You send a short text like, "We need to talk," without providing context. The recipient becomes anxious, assuming the worst.

Effective: You send a text saying, "I'd like to catch up on something important about [specific topic]. When would be a good time to talk?" This provides clarity and reduces unnecessary stress.

Problem-Solution Framework:

- **Problem:** Vague digital messages can cause misunderstandings and emotional distress.

- **Solution:** Use precise, context-rich language to avoid misinterpretation and establish a positive tone.

ཞཞཞ

Professional Scenario: Managing Virtual Team Meetings

Ineffective: During a virtual meeting, you multitask, occasionally glancing at the camera, which makes the team feel unimportant and disengaged.

Effective: You maintain eye contact with the camera, engage with team members by addressing them by name, and summarise their contributions to show attentiveness. This demonstrates respect and creates a more collaborative atmosphere.

Problem-Solution Framework:

- **Problem:** A lack of presence during virtual meetings diminishes engagement and morale.

- **Solution:** Practice active participation by maintaining virtual eye contact, acknowledging input, and staying focused on the discussion.

ଝଝଝ

Personal Scenario: Navigating Social Media Misunderstandings

Ineffective: A friend comments on your social media post, and you respond defensively, saying, "That's not what I meant. Maybe you should reread it." This escalates the situation.

Effective: You reply calmly, "I see how that could be misunderstood. Thanks for pointing it out. Let me clarify." This approach maintains a respectful dialogue and defuses tension.

Problem-Solution Framework:

- **Problem:** Defensive responses on social media can escalate conflicts and harm relationships.

- **Solution:** Use thoughtful, empathetic language to clarify and address misunderstandings without fuelling conflict.

ଝଝଝ

Professional Scenario: Adapting Communication Across Cultures

Ineffective: You schedule a meeting with an international client and immediately dive into business without acknowledging cultural norms for pleasantries. The client feels disrespected and disengaged.

Effective: You start the meeting by acknowledging their cultural preferences, saying, "I hope your week is going well. Before we begin, I'd love to hear your thoughts on [non-business topic]." This builds rapport and demonstrates cultural sensitivity.

Problem-Solution Framework:

- **Problem:** Ignoring cultural nuances can create barriers and misunderstandings in professional relationships.

- **Solution:** Research cultural norms beforehand and adapt your communication style to show respect and understanding.

ะะะ

Personal Scenario: Miscommunication in Group Chats

Ineffective: In a family group chat, you send a joking message that gets misinterpreted as serious. This creates confusion and tension.

Effective: You clarify your tone with an emoji or follow-up message: "Just kidding! ☺ Let's plan something fun soon." This ensures the intended meaning is conveyed and maintains harmony.

Problem-Solution Framework:

- **Problem:** Text-based communication often lacks Non-verbal cues, leading to misinterpretation.

- **Solution:** Use emojis or follow-up messages to clarify tone and intent in casual digital conversations.

ะะะ

Professional Scenario: Overcoming Digital Communication Overload

Ineffective: You bombard your team with emails throughout the day, each covering a different topic. This creates confusion and overwhelms them.

Effective: You consolidate information into a single, well-structured email with clear subject lines and bullet points for action items. This improves clarity and reduces digital fatigue.

Problem-Solution Framework:

- **Problem:** Unstructured or excessive digital communication hinders productivity and clarity.

- **Solution:** Be intentional and organised with digital messages. Prioritise clarity and actionable steps.

&&&

Part 4: Communicating for Lasting Impact

Personal Scenario: Balancing Assertiveness and Compassion

Ineffective: A close friend repeatedly borrows items but doesn't return them. Frustrated, you finally snap and say, "You never return anything! Why do I even bother?"

Effective: You calmly address the situation, saying, "I've noticed a pattern where borrowed items aren't returned. I'd appreciate it if we could work together to ensure things are returned promptly." This balances assertiveness with empathy, preserving the relationship while expressing your concerns.

Problem-Solution Framework:

- **Problem:** Reacting impulsively can strain relationships and hinder effective communication.

- **Solution:** Combine assertiveness with compassion by calmly addressing issues while showing understanding.

જ્જ્જ

Professional Scenario: Leading with Integrity

Ineffective: A team member is concerned about an unrealistic deadline, but you dismiss it, saying, "We all have to work hard as it's part of the job." This undermines their trust in your leadership.

Effective: You acknowledge their concern, saying, "I understand this deadline feels tight. Let's discuss how we can prioritise tasks or redistribute work to make it manageable." This demonstrates integrity by valuing their input and addressing the issue transparently.

Problem-Solution Framework:

- **Problem:** Ignoring concerns erodes trust and demoralises the team.
- **Solution:** Lead with integrity by acknowledging challenges, offering solutions, and fostering open dialogue.

જ્જ્જ

Personal Scenario: Building Resilience in Communication

Ineffective: After a disagreement with a family member, you avoid addressing the issue and let resentment build, straining the relationship.

Effective: You take time to reflect and then approach the family member, saying, "I value our relationship, and I'd like to discuss what happened so we can move forward." This demonstrates resilience and a willingness to repair and strengthen the bond.

Problem-Solution Framework:

- **Problem:** Avoiding difficult conversations can weaken relationships over time.

- **Solution:** Cultivate resilience by addressing issues constructively and focusing on long-term connection.

ଝଝଝ

Professional Scenario: Empowering Others Through Communication

Ineffective: During a team meeting, you assign tasks without seeking input, leaving team members feeling undervalued and disengaged.

Effective: You involve the team in decision-making, saying, "Here's the project scope, how do you think we can best divide these tasks? I'd love to hear your ideas." This empowers team members, fosters collaboration, and builds trust.

Problem-Solution Framework:

- **Problem:** One-way communication stifles collaboration and engagement.
- **Solution:** Empower others by fostering inclusive discussions and valuing their input.

ଝଝଝ

Personal Scenario: Cultivating Inner Dialogue

Ineffective: You internally criticise yourself after a failed attempt, thinking, "I always mess up, I'll never get this right."

Effective: You reframe your inner dialogue, saying, "This didn't work out, but it's a learning opportunity. Next time, I'll approach it differently." This fosters self-compassion and encourages growth.

Problem-Solution Framework:

- **Problem:** Negative self-talk undermines confidence and personal growth.

- **Solution:** Cultivate a positive inner dialogue to build resilience and maintain motivation.

ৡৡৡ

Professional Scenario: Leaving a Legacy Through Communication

Ineffective: You focus solely on results and overlook mentoring or storytelling opportunities to inspire the next generation of leaders.

Effective: You take time to mentor junior colleagues, sharing your experiences and lessons. For example, during a leadership workshop, you say, "When I faced a similar challenge early in my career, this is how I navigated it." This leaves a lasting impact, inspiring and empowering others.

Problem-Solution Framework:

- **Problem:** Focusing only on short-term goals neglects the potential for lasting influence.

- **Solution:** Use storytelling and mentorship to create a legacy through impactful communication.

Pause and reflect on the scenarios that resonate most with you. What changes will you make starting today?

ൠൠൠ

COMMUNICATION SELF-ASSESSMENT: REVISIT YOUR PROGRESS

Now that you have journeyed through this book, it's time to return to the checklist you completed at the beginning. Re-evaluate each question using the same scale from 0 (Never) to 5 (Always). Take a moment to compare your responses from before and after reading.

Notice any shifts in your understanding or approach to communication. Where have you grown? Which areas would you still like to develop? Reflect on these changes as a testament to your growth and a guide for continuing your journey in mastering effective, impactful communication.

- **0** = Never
- **1** = Rarely
- **2** = Occasionally

- **3** = Sometimes
- **4** = Frequently
- **5** = Always

Let's dive in and get a sense of where you are with your communication today after successfully learning the aspects of Communication. Enjoy the process!

1. I feel comfortable sharing my thoughts clearly.

   1   **2**   **3**   **4**   **5**

2. I pay attention to my body language and tone.

   1   **2**   **3**   **4**   **5**

3. I try to understand the emotions behind others' words.

   1   **2**   **3**   **4**   **5**

4. I listen without interrupting or planning my response.

   1   **2**   **3**   **4**   **5**

5. I adjust my communication style to fit different people and situations.

   1   **2**   **3**   **4**   **5**

6. I handle difficult conversations calmly.

   1   **2**   **3**   **4**   **5**

7. I am aware of how my inner dialogue affects my communication.

   1   **2**   **3**   **4**   **5**

8. I stay open, minded and try to understand other perspectives.

   1   **2**   **3**   **4**   **5**

9. I make sure my message is clear and understood.

   1   **2**   **3**   **4**   **5**

10. I seek feedback on my communication and try to improve.

    1   2   3   4   5

11. I see communication as a skill I can always improve.

    1   2   3   4   5

12. I manage my emotions well during conversations.

    1   2   3   4   5

13. I consider the impact of my words before speaking.

    1   2   3   4   5

14. I listen with curiosity, not judgment.

    1   2   3   4   5

15. I use both words and Non-verbal cues to convey my message.

    1   2   3   4   5

SELF-AWARENESS & COMMUNICATION STYLE QUIZ

Instructions: Answer each question by selecting the option that best describes how you usually behave in communication situations. Rate each statement on a scale of 1 to 4:

1 = Rarely   2 = Sometimes 3 = Often   4 = Always

This quiz is a self-reflective tool, not a test, so focus on authenticity. Be honest with yourself as you answer to gain the most valuable insights.

1. I do so confidently when expressing my opinions without dominating the conversation.

2. I prefer listening and gathering information before I share my own views.

3. When someone gives me feedback, I take it calmly and consider it an opportunity to improve.

4. I prioritize finding a solution that benefits both sides in conflicts.

5. I use clear and concise language to ensure my message is well understood.

6. When speaking to others, I consider their perspective and adjust my language accordingly.

7. I make a conscious effort to maintain eye contact and use open body language.

8. If I disagree with someone, I express my thoughts respectfully without avoiding the discussion.

9. When explaining a complex idea, I break it down to make it easier for others to understand.

10. I handle interruptions calmly and redirect the conversation if necessary.

11. I am comfortable asking clarifying questions to ensure we're on the same page.

12. In group settings, I contribute my ideas while also encouraging others to share theirs.

13. I find it easy to put myself in someone else's shoes to understand their perspective.

14. When in disagreement, I listen carefully before responding to avoid misunderstandings.

15. I adjust my tone and approach depending on the person or group I'm addressing.

16. I feel comfortable expressing disagreement constructively.

17. I regularly check in with others to confirm that they understand my point of view.

18. I follow up after discussions to ensure everyone is aligned and clear on the next steps.

19. I am comfortable discussing uncomfortable or sensitive topics when necessary.

20. When communicating, I pay attention to the non-verbal cues of the other person.

Results Guide: Calculate your total score by adding up your responses. Then, compare your total to the style descriptions below to determine your dominant communication style.

64-80 Points – Assertive Style

You are a confident and balanced communicator. You express yourself clearly and value open dialogue. You adapt well to different situations and strive for mutually beneficial outcomes. This balanced approach fosters trust and harmony in relationships. Maintain this approach, as it builds mutual respect and strengthens connections.

48-63 Points – Collaborative Style

You prioritize harmony and inclusivity in communication. You often encourage teamwork and are skilled at gathering diverse perspectives. Your empathy and consideration for others' views are strengths. Continue practicing assertiveness, especially in situations where you need to set clear boundaries or assert your ideas confidently.

32-47 Points – Passive or Analytical Style

You may tend to hold back in conversations, preferring to listen and analyze. This makes you observant and thoughtful, but there is room to practice vocalizing your thoughts more openly. Balancing listening with sharing your insights will help others benefit from your unique perspective and increase your influence in discussions.

Below 32 Points – Reserved or Avoidant Style

You may avoid conflict or strong expressions of your opinions, often preferring to maintain peace. While keeping harmony is beneficial, being overly reserved may limit your influence and contributions. Building confidence in your voice can help others appreciate your perspective and make your communication more impactful.

After discovering your dominant communication style, please take a moment to reflect on where you might want to adapt or strengthen your communication.

Identify one or two areas you'd like to develop and set actionable goals based on your reflection. For example, if you want to practice assertiveness, you could set a goal to express your thoughts more openly in group discussions. Keep reviewing your progress and celebrate small improvements along the way.

Here's a Sample Format for your reference!

- **Goal**: What specific aspect of communication do you want to improve in your relationships?
  - *Example*: "I will listen empathetically and not advise until asked."
- **Action Steps**:
  - Step 1: ____________ 100% Listening
  - Step 2: ____________ Look at the situation from the other person's viewpoint
  - Step 3: ____________ Make the other person feel comfortable and supported
- **Milestones**:
  - 1st Milestone (e.g., After one week/Month): ____________
  - 2nd Milestone (e.g., After three weeks/months): ____________
- **Reflections**:
  - What has changed in your interactions with family or friends?
  - How have you noticed others responding to your efforts?

PROGRESS TRACKER

Instructions for Weekly Tracking

Before you begin, make three additional copies of this progress tracker so you can assess your progress each week for the next month. Mark your responses each week to see how your skills develop over time. Use these copies to reflect on your growth, celebrate improvements, and identify areas to focus on in the coming weeks.

Part 1: Foundations of Communication – Quick Progress Tracker

Instructions: Use this tracker to assess how you integrate the foundational communication skills discussed in Part 1. Based on your week's experience, mark each statement as Yes, Sometimes, or Not Yet.

Statement	Yes	Sometimes	Not Yet
I feel more aware of my communication style.			
I recognize when I'm not actively listening and can adjust my focus.			
I notice and understand Non-verbal cues during conversations.			

Statement	Yes	Sometimes	Not Yet
I practice empathetic listening with friends, family, and colleagues.			
While communicating, I consciously check in on the other person's understanding.			

Part 2: Transforming How You Communicate with Others – Quick Progress Tracker

Instructions: *Reflect on the skills in Part 2. Mark each statement based on your progress this week.*

Statement	Yes	Sometimes	Not Yet
I express my thoughts clearly and intentionally during conversations.			
I approach challenging conversations with openness and respect.			
I am mindful of my body language and tone when communicating.			
I check for mutual understanding in conversations, especially in complex discussions.			
I make an effort to adjust my communication style depending on the needs of the conversation.			

Part 3: Communication in the Modern World – Quick Progress Tracker

Instructions: *Assess your progress on the skills discussed in Part 3. Mark each response according to your weekly experience.*

Statement	Yes	Sometimes	Not Yet
I communicate mindfully and attentively in digital conversations (texts, emails, etc.).			
I remain respectful and open to different perspectives, even when they differ.			
I consider cultural differences and adapt my communication style accordingly.			
I use digital communication tools effectively to convey my message.			
I'm mindful of my tone and words to avoid misunderstandings in digital exchanges.			

DEEPENING LEADERSHIP WITH INTEGRITY

Evaluate and deepen your leadership practices with integrity with the help of the checklist below on a scale of 1 to 5, where:

1 = Rarely

2 = Occasionally

3 = Sometimes

4 = Often

5 = Always

Identify areas where you scored lower and reflect on opportunities for growth.

Checklist Item	1	2	3	4	5
Do I consistently align my actions with my stated values and principles?	☐	☐	☐	☐	☐
2. Do I follow through on commitments, ensuring I deliver on promises?	☐	☐	☐	☐	☐
3. Do I communicate transparently, even when delivering difficult news?	☐	☐	☐	☐	☐
4. Do I prioritise ethical decision-making, even when challenging or costly?	☐	☐	☐	☐	☐
5. Do I take accountability for my mistakes and work to resolve them?	☐	☐	☐	☐	☐

Checklist Item	1	2	3	4	5
6. Do I actively seek and value feedback from my team or peers on my leadership?	☐	☐	☐	☐	☐
7. Do I create an environment where others feel safe to share ideas and concerns?	☐	☐	☐	☐	☐
8. Do I consistently recognise and reward contributions aligned with shared values?	☐	☐	☐	☐	☐
9. Do I foster trust by being approachable and dependable in my interactions?	☐	☐	☐	☐	☐
10. Do I encourage open dialogue and lead by example in demonstrating integrity?	☐	☐	☐	☐	☐

- **Reflection**: Review your responses. Which areas scored lower? Reflect on the possible reasons and what steps you can take to improve. Use the chapter as a guide to revisit concepts and practical strategies.

- **Contemplate**: Think about how your actions align with your values and the impact of your leadership on your team or organisation. Identify specific behaviours to refine.

- **Commit**: Measure your integrity every month using this checklist to track your progress. Focus on one or two areas for improvement and implement small, consistent changes over time.

YOUR GATEWAY TO MASTERING COMMUNICATION

This annexure is designed to be your comprehensive guide to further your learning and mastery of communication. Start with **TED Talks** for quick, impactful insights, delve into **Books** for in-depth understanding, and finally, explore **Research Journals** for scholarly, evidence-based exploration. Each resource offers a unique layer to enhance your journey in communication, leadership, and personal growth.

TED Talks: Start Learning Today

Discover powerful, engaging talks that provide practical communication insights:

1. **Julian Treasure**: *How to Speak So That People Want to Listen*
2. **Celeste Headlee**: *10 Ways to Have a Better Conversation*
3. **Amy Cuddy**: *Your Body Language Shapes Who You Are*
4. **Simon Sinek**: *How Great Leaders Inspire Action*
5. **Brené Brown**: *The Power of Vulnerability*
6. **Shonda Rhimes**: *My Year of Saying Yes to Everything*
7. **Dan Pink**: *The Puzzle of Motivation*
8. **Susan Cain**: *The Power of Introverts*

9. **Caroline Goyder**: *The Surprising Secret to Speaking with Confidence*

10. **Laura Vanderkam**: *How to Gain Control of Your Free Time*

11. **Tim Urban**: *Inside the Mind of a Master Procrastinator*

12. **Elizabeth Gilbert**: *Your Elusive Creative Genius*

13. **Robert Waldinger**: *What Makes a Good Life? Lessons from the Longest Study on Happiness*

14. **Kelly McGonigal**: *How to Make Stress Your Friend*

15. **John Koenig**: *Beautiful New Words to Describe Obscure Emotions*

Books: Dive Deep for In-Depth Knowledge

These books offer a range of insights, from practical tools to leadership strategies:

1. **Stephen R. Covey**: *The 7 Habits of Highly Effective People*

2. **Dale Carnegie**: *How to Win Friends and Influence People*

3. **Marshall B. Rosenberg**: *Nonviolent Communication: A Language of Life*

4. **Chris Voss**: *Never Split the Difference: Negotiating as If Your Life Depended on It*

5. **Susan Scott**: *Fierce Conversations: Achieving Success at Work and in Life One Conversation at a Time*

6. **Sheryl Sandberg**: *Lean In: Women, Work, and the Will to Lead*

7. **Cal Newport**: *Deep Work: Rules for Focused Success in a Distracted World*

8. **Adam Grant**: *Give and Take: Why Helping Others Drives Our Success*

9. **Amy Edmondson**: *The Fearless Organization: Creating Psychological Safety in the Workplace*

10. **Bernard Ferrari**: *Power Listening: Mastering the Most Critical Business Skill of All*

11. **Patti Sanchez and Nancy Duarte**: *Illuminate: Ignite Change Through Speeches, Stories, Ceremonies, and Symbols*

12. **Erica Dhawan**: *Digital Body Language: How to Build Trust and Connection, No Matter the Distance*

13. **Susan Cain**: *Quiet: The Power of Introverts in a World That Can't Stop Talking*

14. **Malcolm Gladwell**: *The Tipping Point: How Little Things Can Make a Big Difference*

15. **Patrick Lencioni**: *The Five Dysfunctions of a Team: A Leadership Fable*

Journals: Research-Oriented Reading

For a deeper academic exploration of communication principles:

1. **Journal of Communication**

2. **Harvard Business Review** (Leadership & Communication Editions)

3. **Communication Monographs**

4. **International Journal of Business Communication**

5. **Journal of Applied Communication Research**

6. **Discourse Studies**

7. **Management Communication Quarterly**

8. **Journal of Intercultural Communication Research**

9. **Corporate Communications: An International Journal**

10. **Nonverbal Behavior Journal**

THE CLOSING NOTE

Thank you for joining me on this journey into the heart of communication. I hope these pages have informed and inspired you to see communication as a powerful personal and professional growth tool. As you continue, remember that each interaction is an opportunity to practice, connect, and build meaningful relationships. Keep this book as a companion to revisit whenever you need a refresher, and may your communication continue to open doors, create opportunities, and enrich your life in ways you may have never anticipated.

I would love to hear your feedback, experiences, or any thoughts you'd like to share. Feel free to email me at jyotsna@jyotsnabidave.com or connect with me on social media. You can find me on,

YouTube: http://www.youtube.com/@JyotsnaBidave

Instagram: https://www.instagram.com/jyotsna_bidave

LinkedIn: www.linkedin.com/in/jyotsna-bidave

Blog: https://jyotsnabidave.com/blog

Let's keep this conversation going!